INVITATION *to* FAITH

IRH Press

Originally published in Japan
as *Shinko no Susume*
- Deichu no Hana, Tomeina Kaze no Gotoku
by IRH Press Co., Ltd., in June 2005.

IRH PRESS
New York

ISBN: 978-1-958655-71-9
Cover Images: © Kotama, igor_tichonow/PIXTA

Printed in Japan

First Edition

INVITATION *to* FAITH

Attain Enlightenment and Give Love

EL CANTARE

RYUHO OKAWA

IRH Press

Contents

CHAPTER TWO

On the World after Death

CHAPTER THREE

What Is Faith?

—Question and Answer Sessions

CHAPTER FOUR

Love Blows Like the Wind

*All chapters compiled in this book are originally lectures recorded in Japanese and later translated in English.

Preface

In this book, *Invitation to Faith*, I have explained the general idea of Happy Science teachings in a clear and simple manner. I believe it will serve as a good religious book.

Chapter One is titled "A Lotus Flower Blooms in the Mud." Here, I have explained how you should understand, contemplate, and practice Buddhist teachings in this modern age of frequent wars, terrorism, and earthquakes. Some of you will be amazed to discover the real meaning of the Lotus Sutra. Indeed, this world may appear dirty like a muddy swamp. However, just as a lotus flower blooms in the mud, everyone can bloom a magnificent flower that is not of this world—a flower of enlightenment—even while living in this seemingly dirty world. This is the point I made in this chapter.

Chapter Two, "On the World after Death," contains important elements that complement one of my previously published Laws series, *The Mystical Laws* (Tokyo: HS Press, 2015). Here, I have provided additional and detailed explanations of the world after death. By reading this chapter together with *The Mystical Laws*, you will get an even better understanding of the afterlife.

Chapter Three, "What Is Faith?" is a selection of Q&A sessions that I gave at grand public lectures. I picked out clear and simple Q&As that focused on the topic of faith. In responding to the audience's questions, I spoke about faith and revealed my fundamental perspective.

Chapter Four, "Love Blows Like the Wind," is a lecture I gave for non-Japanese audiences with our global missionary work in mind. "Love Blows Like the Wind" is also the title of my novel series, which tells the life story of the great hero Hermes. In the lecture, I explained Hermes' thought in relation to Christian teachings to help Western audiences understand it more. I have disclosed the philosophy of Hermes while showing that Happy Science teachings are based on two axes: Buddhist thought and Greek philosophy. Moreover, I explained how Hermes' thought is taught in the current age and how it is related to the Christian society. These were the main points of this lecture. I believe the overseas audiences enjoyed it greatly.

This time, the above lectures were compiled into and published as a single book. I am sure it will be loved by many readers. It is my sincere wish that this book will be read by as many people as possible.

Ryuho Okawa
Master & CEO of Happy Science Group
Spring 2005

CHAPTER ONE

A Lotus Flower Blooms in the Mud

Recorded in Japanese on March 18, 2003
at Happy Science's General Headquarters in Tokyo, Japan.

1

Things Do Not Always Go Your Way in This World

In this chapter, I would like to explain one of Buddhism's core teachings in simple terms by putting it in a modern context.

There are various ways of viewing this world, but ultimately, most people's suffering arises from the fact that things do not always go their way in this world. Of course, we can accomplish things through our effort to a certain extent, within the range of our abilities. However, there are times when we are overwhelmed by a greater force, a greater misfortune, or a greater torrent of hardships that is more than what humans can handle. At such times, most people drown in the sea of pain because they cannot cope with it. This happens at any age. No matter what kind of environment humans strive to create, there will always be people who end up drowning in the waves of suffering.

2

View Yourself and the World from a General Perspective

Humans are selfish in nature

A while ago, there was a rerun of a Japanese TV series called "Oshin," which was very popular back when it was originally aired. The story is set in the days before World War II. It was a time when many people suffered in poverty, and families struggled to feed their children. So, especially in rural areas such as villages in northern Japan, parents sent their children away from home to work so that they could cut down on the number of mouths to feed. The TV series was about the tough life of a girl named Oshin, who was born into such difficult times. Oshin was sent to work as a nanny at a young age, and she sometimes was not fed lunch. As she took care of the baby on her back, she longed to go to school to study. It was a time of such poverty that people struggled simply to survive.

Times have changed since then, and we are now living in an age when there is an abundance of food. More and more children now say that they do not want to go to school or tutoring classes. Even if they go, they are full of complaints because they hate studying or they do not like their school.

Unexpectedly, in times of food shortage, such as during the war-torn period or post-war devastation, people rarely think of committing suicide. They do not need to because death is already so close. Their concerns are about how many days they can survive without food, so they would not need to take the trouble to kill themselves. Rather, it is in times of abundance—when there is plenty of food and people do not starve to death—that more and more people choose to take their lives because of some kind of dissatisfaction. This is, indeed, a strange phenomenon.

Happy Science has been carrying out a suicide prevention campaign since the beginning of 2003. However, newspapers and other media outlets have been reporting cases of what is called "internet suicide." This is a type of suicide where people who want to kill themselves connect over the internet, make a plan to meet, and then commit suicide together in places like the mountains. I suppose they feel lonely to die alone, so three to four people get together and die together. There was another news story about a person who committed suicide by burning charcoal and inhaling carbon monoxide fumes. Charcoal was commonly used at home in the past, but it is rarely used today. I was surprised to learn that someone had taken their life using such an old method. People who turn to suicide likely feel dissatisfied with life and find no joy in living in this world.

In times of food shortage, most people are desperate to live each day, and their thoughts are far from committing suicide. They would even think of buying rice from the black market or stealing food so that they could somehow survive. During the time when not everyone could attend school, people yearned for the opportunity to study. But in times when food is plentiful and schooling is a matter of course, people say they do not want to study or attend school. Some even commit suicide because they find no meaning in life or feel mistreated by others. This is, indeed, a strange phenomenon.

When caught up in their own subjective view, people fail to realize how blessed they are. Unless they look at themselves from a broader, more general standpoint, they cannot realize how much has already been given to them. Humans are, indeed, selfish by nature. If you compare your life to the lives of those who live in a harsher environment or in deeper poverty, you can see how fortunate your circumstances are. Yet, some people cannot grasp this. Instead, they look at the world from a self-centered lens and may even take their lives impulsively over small matters. This shows how difficult it is to step outside a subjective viewpoint and look at yourself objectively.

Instead of only focusing on your surroundings, you should broaden your perspective and look at things from a global perspective. Please look at the world, the society you live in, your school, your family, and yourself from a broader perspective. It is important that you consider things more carefully in this way.

The same environment cannot be provided for everyone

We are now living in an age when diverse values and environments coexist. In India and parts of Africa, many people still live in houses made of mud. They press cow dung patties onto walls to dry in the sun and use them as fuel. Meanwhile, there are countries that manufacture missiles worth millions of dollars each and fire them at enemies. It is, indeed, a peculiar era when people with different life standards and things of different developmental levels coexist. If a deadly natural disaster were to occur and all advanced nations were to sink beneath the ocean, leaving only the developing countries intact, people in the future would probably think we all lived in mud houses and used cow dung for fuel. For instance, people 2,000 years from now would likely see our entire age this way if only those developing regions remained.

In this modern age, a wide variety of things coexist, and people's sense of values has become more complex. So, if you consider happiness and unhappiness from a global perspective, in other words, from the viewpoint of billions of people living across the globe, you will come to see how difficult it is to satisfy the needs of all people and make them all happy. I want you to be aware of this. Even if we wish for everyone to be happy, that is not an easy task. It is impossible to provide everyone with an environment, a society, or a position that will satisfy them all.

No matter how modernized a country is or how prosperous a company is, there will always be different levels of positions. While an employee may be promoted to president or vice-president and make high-level decisions, another employee is in charge of simple tasks such as sending out mail or filing documents. People in charge of filing documents may not be enjoying their work, but they do not realize that some are doing even less enjoyable jobs, such as cleaning the office floor after everyone goes home. People tend to forget that many people in this world are doing unpleasant and tiresome work.

You may wish for everyone to be happy, but if you define happiness as a specific lifestyle, appearance, or position, you can never make everyone happy. This is because it is impossible to provide everyone with the same position or environment. Each person is given a different role and circumstances. You cannot share the same family relationship, gender, age, or income as others, and social status will naturally differ as well. You cannot make a claim that people who join a specific company will become happy, while those who do not will all become unhappy. Happiness and unhappiness will visit the lives of both those who enter the company and those who do not. The same applies to schools. You cannot say that attending a certain school will make students full of joy, while being rejected will make them all miserable. Whether you succeed or fail to enter a particular company or school, you will all experience both happiness and unhappiness. In this way, there are all kinds of cases.

Therefore, it is impossible for everyone to be happy as long as they believe that they can only be satisfied and happy when they meet the objective conditions of happiness. You need to be aware of this. Of course, it is extremely important to strive to create an environment or outcome that everyone considers good; this in itself is a precious effort. However, this does not mean that everyone will be satisfied and happy by achieving those goals. As long as people seek earthly happiness, it is virtually impossible for all of them to be satisfied.

Some may seek promotion or power, but once they achieve it, they will face new challenges. You may think that worldly success brings you happiness, but the higher your position, the heavier your responsibility will be. Those in higher positions must make painful decisions or deal with dire situations sometimes. While working in lower positions is certainly tough, those in higher positions are facing difficulties of a different nature.

3
Earthquakes and Wars Are Beyond a Person's Control

Earthquakes bring misfortune to both good and bad people

Big earthquakes are one example of external factors that are beyond a person's control. Sometimes, an earthquake brings death to thousands or tens of thousands of people. Unfortunately, it cannot choose to attack only bad people and avoid good ones; it doesn't work that way. In the same way, fires caused by earthquakes cannot choose which houses to avoid. It is sad, but when disasters occur, both good and bad people will likely suffer misfortunes, although the extent of the damage may differ.

When the Great Hanshin Earthquake struck Japan in 1995, many Happy Science members worked very hard to help the victims, and we felt relieved to see positive results coming out of it. But I still remember a scene I glimpsed on the TV news at the time. The news was broadcasting the devastating scenes of Kobe City, where many people were crying around their collapsed houses, searching for their missing family members who might be buried under the rubble. That is when I noticed something glint. It was the RO pendant (a holy object of Happy Science) worn by a young woman who appeared to be in her twenties. She seemed to be the daughter of a family that lived in one of the collapsed houses. It looked like she was trying to find her family. Watching on TV, I was reminded that some of the Happy Science members have also lost their family members in this earthquake, and I felt deeply saddened. This memory has stayed with me after many years. Her entire neighborhood appeared completely destroyed, so it would have been impossible for the earthquake to spare only her house. Of course, I'm certain the spirit group of Happy Science in the heavenly world went to save the souls of her deceased family members. But sadly, some earthly misfortunes are simply unavoidable. I can only say it was fortunate that the young woman with Happy Science faith was at least safe. Thus, people cannot avoid sufferings caused by natural disasters like earthquakes, which are beyond human control.

War repeatedly breaks out

There are also times when a war breaks out. This is another tragedy we can do very little about as individuals. No matter how many people oppose war, it still happens; it cannot be helped. Sometimes, a war breaks out due to the decisions made by those in power or for political purposes, so even a majority vote cannot stop it. What is more, some wars break out based on a deep insight into how things should unfold in the flow of history.

In 2003, for example, there was the Iraq War. When President George W. Bush declared war on Iraq, 70 to 80 percent of people in the world were against it, as were many Americans. They were likely exhausted from people dying from war, which is understandable.

The Gulf War in 1991 was reported as a great victory for the coalition. When I happened to see a picture of the annihilated Iraqi tank unit in the suburbs of Basra in Iraq, it was truly a tragic situation; it almost looked like a massacre. Some reports said that the Iraqi casualties numbered over a hundred thousand people. From this, I learned that the difference in civilization and technology between countries will also create a significant difference in war outcomes. Even though a hundred Iraqi tanks were destroyed, not even a single US tank was harmed; the American force was extremely strong. The American units used depleted uranium ammunition that tore through the armored plating of Iraqi tanks and exploded inside them. Americans were using advanced technology. They also used Apache helicopters, which were made to attack tanks from the sky. In contrast, Iraqi tanks were old and underdeveloped compared to the U.S. tanks; as expected, they were completely destroyed in what almost seemed like a total massacre. Since it was an extremely horrific sight, the U.S. government controlled information and prohibited any photos that captured the battlefield scenes from circulating in Europe and America. As for the Iraqis, they did not want their defeat to be shown to the public, so they did not release any photos either. Consequently, both sides turned a blind eye to the brutal fact.

War is truly cruel, yet it repeatedly breaks out. Countries fight wars even though no one wants to die. One of the reasons for this is that they are trying to deter bigger wars or even more severe tragedies from happening in the future. Ultimately, this is the reason President George W. Bush insisted on attacking Iraq. He suspected that Saddam Hussein was pulling the strings on Osama Bin Laden, who led the 911 attack on the World Trade Center and the Pentagon in September 2001, which killed thousands of people. Bush thought that as long as Iraq was left as it was, terrorism would continue for more than 10 or 20 years. He believed that terrorism would never end as long as the whole country was supporting it, and therefore, Iraq—the big boss—could not be forgiven.

Consequently, however, it triggered wars of mutual vengeance. I am afraid that various conflicts will continue to arise between the two sides. To overcome mutual vengeance, Buddhism has already taught 2,500 years ago that conflict will never end unless you abandon hatred.

4

The Work of Religion Is to Save People's Souls

War brings casualties to both sides

While people can solve problems rationally to a certain extent, they have little power over issues that go beyond human effort. Even God can rarely stop the wars that occur in this world. Because human beings are given freedom in this world, they also have the freedom and the right to engage in wars. That is why wars never seem to end. So, ultimately, the work of religion is to save people's souls.

In truth, there are no winners or losers in war. In the Gulf War, countless Iraqi people died. As for the American soldiers, although it was reported that only about a hundred of them were killed, tens of thousands went through heavy suffering after the war. They were diagnosed with the "Gulf War syndrome" and hospitalized. At first, the syndrome was believed to have been caused by Iraqi biological weapons, but the truth turned out to be that these soldiers inhaled the depleted uranium particles of their own weapons, which damaged their nervous system. The United States tried hard to conceal this fact. In the Vietnam War, too, many American soldiers suffered from post-war traumas. In this way, wars inflict a considerable amount of damage on both sides, so it is essential for religion to save the souls of the victims.

Long ago, in Shakyamuni Buddha's time, some kings pledged devotion to Buddha. Among them were the kings of the Kosala Kingdom and the Magadha Kingdom. Even though they were both Buddha's disciples, they had military forces and sometimes fought against each other in a war. Politics has its own logic, so the two kings did not stop fighting, although they believed in the same teachings. Some Buddhist scriptures hand down Buddha's thoughts on war, which state that "the responsibility of war essentially weighs on the king, as he is the one who leads the war." Buddha said, "The king shall take the responsibility for whether the war was good or evil; the blame does not lie with the soldiers who served in the army as their duty. The decision of the top is what matters. The king who led the war must be held accountable for whether the war was good or evil."

But in reality, American soldiers, for instance, who fought in the Vietnam War under the order of the president suffered tremendous post-war trauma that drove them to insanity. They suffered from recurring nightmares and visions of killing a considerable number of the Vietcong guerrillas who looked just like the civilians. So, although the people who serve in the army are not responsible for the war, they cannot escape the suffering that comes with it. They can hardly forget the horrifying experience of killing many people, and those painful scars will certainly be etched deep into their souls. No one would want to go through such a painful experience if possible.

Religions must consider people's suffering

During the Iraq War, the Japanese government stood firmly on the side of the U.S. This was probably because they were more concerned about North Korea than Iraq. Japan will be in trouble if it has to deal with North Korea alone in case it fires missiles at Japan. Japan needs the U.S. support, so it cannot change its stance. Since politics has its own logic, it is acceptable for a person who stands in a leadership position to choose the course of action they believe is right.

I must admit that religion is weak in solving practical issues, so it must at least think about saving the minds or souls of people. Religions must consider the sorrow of the survivors of war as well as the suffering of the deceased.

The atomic bombings on Hiroshima and Nagasaki each killed around ten thousand people, and their bereaved families suffered heavily for a very long time. During the

Gulf War, many Iraqi soldiers were killed in Basra, and since they, too, had their own families, their family members will have to experience pain for decades to come. As for America after the attack on the World Trade Center, the families of the victims suffered through severe pain and hardship.

Each and every person creates new karma as they go through struggles and sufferings in the course of their life. Each person's soul training in life intertwines with that of another in countless ways to turn a new page in human history.

5

Live Like a Lotus Flower that Blooms in the Mud

Be determined to bloom your own flower, no matter the circumstances

There are many things in this world that do not go the way we want. Even when someone with good intentions aims to achieve something good, they are not always supported by the majority. In order to stop war from occurring, people came up with the electoral system, but some problems just cannot be solved by voting. Since they cannot be resolved through elections or conferences, they inevitably lead to conflict. This is the way the world works.

When you look around the world, you will find many seeds of unhappiness everywhere. Some of you may believe that people cannot be happy unless all those seeds are eliminated, and you may actually try to remove them and realize paradise in this world. However, that is nearly impossible. The earthly world we live in is a place of many conflicts, destruction, hatred, jealousy, vengeance, anger, and insanity. It is also a world of survival of the fittest and is an extremely tough place to live in. We need to accept this fact as it is, and at the same time, strive to find the meaning of why we are born into this world and the reason we are living in this world. This is an extremely important attitude. Buddhism explains this by using the analogy of lotus flowers that bloom in mud.

Perhaps, you have seen lotus flowers blooming in a swamp or a pond. Those swamps or ponds are all muddy. The lotus stem does not grow out of clear water with white sand or pebbles beneath it, but out of dark and muddy water. Everyone finds the water filthy and foul-smelling. Yet, the lotus stem grows upward to the surface and blooms with white, red, and other colorful flowers. A single lotus flower will make you feel as if you are in heaven or paradise. Since ancient times, lotus flowers have always bloomed in swamps or filthy places where garbage would be dumped. Buddhist monks looked at these flowers with adoration, as they hoped to live like those pure flowers that bloom out of dirt.

The official name of the Lotus Sutra is "The Wonderful Dharma of the Lotus Sutra." The lotus flower is a metaphor for the True Dharma. First, you must understand that the world is full of suffering, and in a sense, it is a world of agonizing cries. People are really struggling, and they are suffering from the pain of not getting what they want. What is worse, some people are even actively harming themselves or causing themselves pain. The truth is, no matter how sincerely or purely you live your life, misfortune is sometimes inevitable. For example, you may lose your partner in a traffic accident, or your parents may get divorced at a time when you are determined to focus on your studies. Today, many children become twisted in their minds because their parents get a divorce, die in a traffic accident, or fail in business and go bankrupt. As a result, they often commit immoral acts or become delinquents. I understand that these children have enough reasons to end up like that. However, we must not forget that unfortunate circumstances or situations have always been around in every age. We must also know that this world is not a beautiful, perfect world that continues for eternity. Even if we are in a happy situation now, it can easily crumble. From the spiritual eyes, or in the eyes of heavenly beings like bodhisattvas and angels, this earthly world looks like a mere muddy pond. What truly matters is how you will let your own flower—an innocent flower like the lotus flower—bloom as you live in this world.

It is possible to let your flower blossom under any circumstance. Some people bloom their flowers as they work in first-rate companies, while others bloom magnificent flowers as they strive in medium-sized or small companies. The same applies to those who attend schools. There are both prestigious schools and so-called bottom-rate schools, but even in bottom-rate schools, some students study hard, develop their abilities, and bloom their flowers magnificently.

Misfortune can also befall at home. One of your family members may fall ill or become disabled in an accident. Your siblings may die young due to an illness or accident, or perhaps one of your parents, or even both of your parents, may die. There are also other painful situations, such as having to flee your home at night because your family is unable to pay off a huge debt. Even so, be determined to bloom your own flower no matter the circumstances, just like the lotus flower that blooms out of a swamp. Strive to live with a pure heart and selflessly. If you live with this determination, you will surely bloom your own flower. The flower may be big or small, but the size does not matter. Please understand that the lotus flower blooms from a muddy pond. If you are having a hard time understanding my words, I suggest you go and see a pond where lotus flowers bloom at least once. You will find heavenly flowers growing straight upward out of a dirty swamp.

Follow the road of enlightenment Shakyamuni Buddha sought

To live like the lotus flower is also the road of enlightenment that Shakyamuni Buddha sought to follow. Here is what he taught:

You cannot purify this world completely and make it a perfect place. However, you, too, can let your own flower bloom in this world, just as lotus flowers bloom out of muddy water. It means you can attain your own enlightenment in the given environment. You cannot change your environment. You cannot erase all the misfortunes you experienced in the past. However, even if people are born into similar kinds of unfortunate circumstances, not all of them fall into the depths of misery. There should be a way for you to polish your mind, seek your path, and bloom your own flower in the given environment. This should be possible for everyone.

This kind of enlightenment is attainable. Letting a beautiful flower bloom in your given situation, circumstances, or environment—this is your enlightenment. In this sense, it is true to say that everyone has Buddha nature within and that they all have a chance to become a buddha. This does not mean that they can become the Buddha who can preach the Laws to save the world, but it is possible for everyone to bloom their own flower in their own circumstances or their own muddy swamp. Never forget to walk on this road to enlightenment.

I would also like to remind you not to be so greedy. Do not hold onto excessive earthly desires. Rather, you should have an "It's enough" mind and be content with what you have been given. Find the way to happiness in the effort of blooming your flower beautifully, no matter what kind of circumstances or adversities you may find yourself in. Just because you have attained all the objective conditions of a "good" life does not mean you can be happy. Even among those who live in enviable and idealistic environments, many are empty in their hearts and are gloomy inside. On the other hand, there are a lot of people who are shining brightly even as they live in a humble environment. Buddhism teaches that it is important to aim for this brilliance and actually attain it.

When you look at your surroundings, the way you have lived so far, or your current state of mind, you may think you have been living in a swamp. Even so, strive to bloom the flower of your enlightenment, no matter how small it may be. Please do not focus only on worldly consequences and believe that you are happy as long as you are blessed with a good worldly environment. *Let your own flower bloom, no matter what kind of environment you are in.* This is the answer to your "workbook of life" as I often teach: "Life is like a workbook of problems to be solved." I hope that you will aspire to bloom your own flower.

CHAPTER TWO

On the World after Death

Recorded in Japanese on November 28, 2001
at Happy Science's General Headquarters in Tokyo, Japan.

1
People Who Do Not Believe in the World after Death

People's responses about their religious faith vary depending on how the question is phrased

Now that Happy Science has grown into a large religious organization, I often give lectures on the premise that the other world exists. But in reality, there are still a lot of people in this world who do not believe in the afterlife. So in this chapter, I will give a simple talk aimed at those who are unsure of what happens after death, those who do not believe in the afterlife, and those who are beginners to Buddha's Truth.

Based on a survey conducted on Japanese people, more than half of them answered "yes" when they were asked whether they believed in something religious. However, this percentage will change depending on whether the question is phrased in an affirmative or negative way. Let us say you want to conduct a survey on people's beliefs in the afterlife. Depending on how you phrase the question, the percentage of people who believe in the afterlife will change from 50 to 30 percent, or even 20 percent. For example, if you ask

Japanese people, "Do you have faith?" fewer people will answer "yes." But if you rephrase it and ask them, "Do you want to visit the graves of your ancestors?" more people will answer "yes." This shows that many Japanese people are confused about their own spiritual beliefs. On one hand, they seem to instinctively believe in the existence of the afterlife despite only having a vague understanding of it, but on the other hand, they are struggling to get their heads around it since they cannot explain the afterlife with the knowledge they learned.

Then, what about the Christian countries, where more people are said to have religious faith compared to Japan? Although roughly 95 percent of the population is registered to a church and people are more or less associated with religious faith, only five percent of them actually practice their faith. Those who believe in heaven and hell, or an afterlife of some kind, probably amount to 60 to 70 percent of the overall population. These are the realistic numbers.

In Japan, a large number of people deny or doubt the existence of the other world, at least on their surface consciousness level. The root of the problem probably lies in Japan's postwar education, which has been heavily based on science.

Materialists only believe in things that can be measured with a "ruler"

Modern science has mainly developed in the last 200 years or so. On the other hand, religion has a history of more than several thousand years, as you can tell by looking at world religions that have been handed down to this day. So, it is practically impossible for science to assess religion, which has been around long before science developed.

When I talk with people who think scientifically and do not believe in the afterlife and the Spirit World, such as scientists and materialists, I get an impression that they are holding a 12-inch ruler and saying, "I won't believe in anything that cannot be measured with this ruler." But can you measure the expanse of the sky with a ruler, for example? Theoretically speaking, perhaps you can, but it sounds like a hopeless attempt. Can you measure the circumference of the Earth with a ruler? I guess you can theoretically, but no one would take on such a backbreaking task.

People who say that they cannot believe in the afterlife based on scientific thinking are similar to those who are trying to measure the sky with a ruler. No words can describe how meaningless this attempt is. To put it differently, these people are saying, "I usually walk on the ground with my own two feet, so I wouldn't believe in anything that is said to exist on the other side of the ocean unless I could actually walk there and see it myself." Even if they are told that there is a continent called Australia across the ocean south of Japan, they would say, "Unless I can walk there, I cannot believe it exists." This is how materialists sound to me.

It is written in the Bible that Jesus Christ walked on the surface of a lake. But even so, he would not walk across the surface of the ocean to get to Australia from Japan. If he were to go that far, people would suggest that he take a ship or a plane instead. In fact, the very act of crossing the ocean by ship or airplane is an act of faith. Those who have never crossed the ocean by ship will probably find it hard to believe it when they are told, "This ship will take you to Australia." They could be shown various pictures and the map of Australia, and be told they can get to Australia in a certain number of days on a ship that travels at a certain number of knots, but they will probably remain doubtful.

Until just a few hundred years ago, people believed that there was a steep cliff at the edge of the Earth and the ocean fell off it like a gigantic waterfall, with nothing else beyond it. People with this worldview would naturally doubt that they can really reach Australia on a ship.

Similarly, those who have never boarded an airplane would feel that flying on a "metal object" is pretty much an act of faith. Since they cannot believe that an airplane can take them to a foreign country, they will start by questioning whether a metal object can really fly in the first place. Even when told, "Just look up and you'll see one flying," they still raise doubts, saying, "But that one might not actually be made of metal." When they are told, "You can see it flying on TV," they will retort, "That might be a fake video," and when they are told, "Some people have actually flown across the ocean to another country and came back on an airplane," they will say, "They might be telling a lie." When you begin to doubt everything in this way, you really cannot believe that one can fly to another country on an airplane. In reality, people who have never boarded an airplane often say, "I'm scared of flights. There is no way such a thing can fly in the sky. I don't trust it!"

You cannot have a further conversation with someone who says, "I don't believe in the existence of a place unless I can walk there." You will be stuck thinking, "Since we cannot walk over the ocean, how can I convince him of that place?" Some people say that they only believe in things that give the same results multiple times and across all people. They even believe that this reflects a scientific or empirical research attitude. But this is the same as insisting, "I do not believe in anything that cannot be measured by a ruler," or "I will not believe in the existence of a place unless I can walk there." These people are proud of the fact that they are not easily persuaded, so it is quite difficult to convince them of anything.

Japanese school education avoids the topic of religion

Some people have a hard time believing in the fact that life continues after death, and there are even those who discourage others from believing in the afterlife. To them, the world of religion probably seems like the world from an old folk tale, a spooky world from *Nihon Ryoiki* (A collection of Buddhist tales written around 1,000 years ago in Japan), or a world of vengeful spirits from the Heian period (798-1185). Or they may see religious teachings as mere philosophies people had in ancient times, such as the Jomon and Yayoi periods (ca. 14,000 BC to 300 BC and ca. 300 BC to 250 AD, respectively). Indeed, the founders of world religions are mostly from ancient times, which are briefly equivalent to those periods in Japanese history. So, people nowadays probably consider religion as something archaic. They perceive the spiritual views of religious founders to be at the same level as primitive scientific technology, such as kindling fire and making earthenware pottery. That is why they think that religious concepts are difficult for modern people like them to believe.

The majority of Japanese people think of religion in the way I have explained above. This is because Japanese school education avoids the topic of religion altogether. Religious education is excluded from the elementary to middle school curriculum, which is compulsory education; neither is it part of high school and university curricula. Some universities offer courses on religious studies, but students who take them often end up becoming atheists. This is because they have a strong tendency to study religion logically and objectively, while remaining nonreligious. They try to analyze it without getting their emotions involved, as if conducting fieldwork. That is why when students study religion seriously, they often end up losing their faith in God.

What is more, Indian philosophy has also become considerably materialistic, much like modern Western philosophy. This is indeed a pitiful situation. Although there are universities that study psychic phenomena, it is very rare, and most of the students who have studied there are unlikely to find a job after graduation. Currently, spirituality is only taught in such places.

2
Faith Will Give You Great Power

Life in this world is a kind of test

People who say they do not know or believe in the world after death probably think, "If there really is such a world and if God or Buddha truly exists, it would be too unkind of Him to make it so unclear. If a world like that really does exist, then He would surely make it more obvious to humans. But since it is not, it means it doesn't exist. We cannot even confirm it by experiment, so it is not worth believing in it."

However, there is a good reason why the existence of the other world is not made obvious to everyone. It is because this world we live in, or the decades of our life, is a kind of test.

Humans come from a spiritual world, which is the true world, the Real World, and dwell in physical bodies to live in this material world. We are being tested on how deeply we can understand and grasp the spiritual views on life as we live in this material world, and how much of God's teachings—that we learned in the past reincarnations—we can deeply understand and put into practice in this lifetime. People accumulate various kinds of experiences in life, which are all part of a test. When the test finishes, or in other words, when your life in this world comes to an end, you will find out the truth about the spiritual world. Once the test is over, your whole life will be reviewed and graded. Until then, the answers will be hidden from you for several decades.

People may say, "If there really is a Spirit World and if God or Buddha really exists, it is very unkind of Him to keep it hidden from us." However, this is the same as complaining during an exam that the answers are not printed on the test, or that the supervisors are being cold for not giving them any hints, for not allowing them to use textbooks, or for not giving them the answers. But of course, these people will simply be told, "It is your job to solve the exam questions in one to two hours. Once the exam is over, it will be marked and returned to you. For the time being, I cannot tell you the answers."

In real life, you may sometimes meet a person who is kind enough to give you hints to solve your problems. Having Happy Science books with you may be like taking an open-book exam. Although we are not given the answers, we are allowed to search and look for hints in the dictionaries with our own effort.

Life is a kind of test, so not all the answers will be revealed to you. However, you will be provided with many clues to solve your problems during the course of your life. Many chances are prepared for you to awaken to the Truth.

Gain a new worldview through believing

As you live in this world, you are tested to see what you will choose in a life full of possibilities and what kinds of ideas and philosophies you will develop or reap as the fruit of your life. Then, after you die, you will find out whether you have earned a perfect score, a passing grade, or a fail. At that time, you will often learn that the worldly values—such as what is considered as success and failure or high status and low status in this world—become completely reversed in the other world.

The high spirits in the Spirit World remain confident and calm, no matter how many people in this world doubt the existence of the Spirit World, are skeptical about religion, or even persecute religion. This is because they know that everyone will eventually pass away. Even if a person insists, "I don't believe in the afterlife!" and makes a big fuss over it, they will face the truth in several years or decades; everything will become obvious to them after death. Sooner or later, humans will die, and they will inevitably experience the spiritual world for themselves.

People on earth may complain that the exam questions are too hard, but the high spirits in the Spirit World will continue to watch over them quietly until the bell rings to signal the end of the exam. Some people may point at a person who is breezing through the questions and say, "This is outrageous! You must be cheating." But the rule is that each person must solve the problems on their own. Whether you can understand or believe in this truth will show what kind of person you are, just like how a litmus paper indicates the nature of a solution.

Knowing about the world after death gives you tremendous power. If you also believe in it, you will gain an even greater power. The act of believing is the equivalent of flying on an airplane or traveling on a ship to go abroad; it comes with risk, but it will take you on a great journey. By traveling to an unknown land or an unknown world, you can gain a whole new worldview. On the other hand, without faith, you will only see and experience the world you can reach on foot.

3
The Meaning Behind Near-Death Experiences

There are many reported cases of near-death experiences

In the last two to three decades, medical scientists have published all kinds of research on near-death experience. Today, near-death experiences—including those of hospice patients—have become a common topic of medical research, and fewer people outright deny them. Although doctors remain hesitant to fully accept them, they are starting to acknowledge their possibility, which is why they have begun studying them. However, they do not yet connect near-death experiences with religion.

According to medical research, there are thousands or even tens of thousands of reported cases of out-of-body experiences or astral projections. When people lose consciousness as a result of a traffic accident, heart attack, or brain disease, for example, and their heart stops beating, they often experience their soul leaving their physical body. There are various patterns of this experience, but in many cases, their spirit body slips out of the physical body from somewhere around their head after cardiac arrest. Then, they look down on their own body lying on the hospital bed in the ICU, as they float midair near the ceiling, six to ten feet above the bed. During this time, they do not feel any pain and are in a very peaceful state. Below them, they can see doctors, nurses, and their family members gathering around their bed and discussing whether they are dead or not, or preparing for emergency treatment. When they look down at their physical body lying on the bed, they see many medical tubes inserted into it, which is an awful sight. So they shout, "Please stop!" But unfortunately, no one can hear them.

Some patients come back to life after 30 minutes to an hour, or even longer, and share with others what they saw and experienced while they were away from this world. Many cases of such near-death experiences have been reported.

Out-of-body experience and the tunnel experience

Each person goes through a different near-death experience, but they all share a similar pattern. In most cases, people feel their soul leaving their body or something going out of their body after their heart stops beating.

On the issue of brain death, Happy Science teaches that a person is not dead as long as their heart keeps beating. In fact, there is a close relationship between cardiac arrest and out-of-body experience; cardiac arrest is a go-sign for the soul to leave the body. It is difficult for the soul to leave the body while the heart is still beating, but it can easily do so once the heart stops beating.

After the soul slips out of the body from somewhere around the head, it usually stays afloat nearby, such as near the body or the ceiling. If the soul grows curious and gets too close to look at its physical body, it will often be pulled back inside. During the out-of-body experience, the soul is connected to its physical body at the back of the head by what is called the silver cord, which looks like a silver thread. Some people have actually seen it during their out-of-body experience; if they are calm enough, they will notice the silver cord being connected to their physical body. Those who have had multiple out-of-body experiences and calmly observed their surroundings will learn that the soul is connected to the physical body via the silver cord. Some have even seen a spirit come from the other world and try to sever the silver cord, just like how doctors cut umbilical cords. So these people have shouted, "No! Don't cut the cord! I won't be able to come back to life if you cut it!" It seems they intuitively know that they will not be revived once their silver cord is cut.

Oftentimes, during a near-death experience, the person's soul is observing the situation from above, near the ceiling of the hospital room. If the person got into a traffic accident and is transported in the ambulance, their soul follows the body by floating above the ambulance. The soul cannot leave its physical body completely while it is still connected to the body via the silver cord, so it lingers around. During that time, the soul is able to understand what the people around them are saying and thinking. For example, it can hear what the nurses are whispering in the room next door or what the doctors are thinking inside their heads. Besides that, they may also see various other scenes of this world.

Thus, the soul tends to hover around the body without making much sense of what is happening to it. But after a while, it usually undergoes the so-called "tunnel experience." The soul first sees a single black dot appear in front of them, and while it wonders what that might be, the black dot quickly spreads widely like an ink stain and begins to look like a black tunnel. The dot continues to grow in size until it engulfs the soul. Many people have experienced this. Apparently, the tunnel experience only occurs when the soul travels to the Spirit World after leaving the physical body.

Lots of people who had this experience have said they heard an unpleasant roaring sound or buzzing sound as they entered the tunnel. At the same time, there are also those who did not hear anything and said that it was completely silent throughout the tunnel experience. It is reported that most people see a round-shaped tunnel, while some see it square-shaped. They usually move through the tunnel as if they are flying, but in the case of infants, they sometimes crawl through it.

People have given various accounts of how it felt when moving through the tunnel. Their descriptions sound very similar to how a person would feel when they go through a wormhole, as described in cosmology. In cosmology, it is said that you can leap through time and space by going through a wormhole. As a matter of fact, souls are indeed traveling from the third dimension to the fourth dimension during the tunnel experience, so this is probably a sensation that a soul experiences when it travels to another dimension. But this is not to say that there is a tunnel in space like the one you find in this world. Each person has described the tunnel differently, which shows that a tunnel does not have a fixed shape but is a kind of wormhole or an opening that is temporarily formed to allow a spirit to travel through time and space to reach another dimension.

Once the soul exits the tunnel, it usually sees an extremely bright light. Some said that it was a white light so blinding that they could not keep their eyes open, while others said that it was not so blinding, although the light was hundreds of times brighter than the sunlight. People said various things, but in any case, the majority said they witnessed a bright white light. At this stage, their vision is still hazy from the light, but they can vaguely see that someone has appeared before them. Many said that it was God, but it is quite unlikely for God to appear in front of everyone. So, in most cases, it is likely to be the person's guardian spirit or a guiding angel with a slightly higher spiritual grade than their guardian spirit. A guiding angel will come down to accompany the soul to the other world.

The River Styx

Eventually, the soul will arrive at the so-called River Styx. Japanese people, especially, witness this river during a near-death experience. Being led by a guiding angel, the soul will walk through the light to reach a vast flower field. All kinds of flowers are blooming in the field, such as rapeseed flowers, cosmos, and daisies. They look similar to the beautiful gardens we find in parks in this world. You can also see a clean river running through it. The river symbolizes the boundary between life and death. It is said that once you cross it, there is no turning back. Many people who have had a near-death experience said that they turned back before fully crossing the river, or they did not cross the river at all.

In fact, the silver cord is cut off when the soul fully crosses over the river. Whether the soul should cross the river or not is decided through a discussion between the soul and the spirits who are from the other side of the river. People have testified that as soon as their soul left their body, their deceased grandmother or grandfather came to greet them, while many others have said they met their deceased family members after they traveled through the tunnel and entered the world of light. Usually, the spirits of the deceased are on the other side of the River Styx, and they either talk to you from the other side or come over to your side to talk. They beckon you to cross over to the other side, and you are sometimes tempted to just follow them because you feel so peaceful and comfortable in the other world.

Meanwhile, in the earthly world, your family members have gathered around your hospital bed, begging you not to die. The wife may be clinging to the husband in the hospital bed and crying, "You can't die yet! Our kids are still so young!" If the husband's soul in the other world hears her voice from behind, he may be pulled back into his body. But if the family does not make it to the hospital in time, he may cross the River Styx and pass away.

The patients in the hospital have been suffering from illness for a long time or enduring excruciating pain from an injury, but in the other world, they feel peaceful and comfortable and are embraced by warmth and love. So, most of them think, "Ah, how pleasant this world is. I wouldn't mind living here. How easy my life would be if I crossed over. I don't want to go back anymore." That is why, if the family members do not make it to the patients' bedside when their souls are being beckoned to the other world, they will cross over to the other side without hesitation and pass away. Usually, when a person is nearing death, their family and relatives are called over. This is partly because they can still persuade the patient not to die yet. So, if the family arrives on time, the person may return to this world and continue to live.

Throughout history, there have been instances of people coming back to life during the wake before their funeral. This is because their silver cords are still connected to their bodies. Their souls are unsure of what is happening and wander nearby, so if they are told very strongly that they still have a mission to fulfill in this world, they could sometimes come back to life. They may be told by their deceased family members who came from the other side of the River Styx that it is still too early for them to return to the other world. Their late fathers, mothers, grandfathers, grandmothers, or siblings may tell them, "It's still a little too early for you to come here. You should live and hang in there a little longer." The patients' souls feel so peaceful that they feel like crossing over, but sometimes they are told by their deceased relatives not to come since they still have some important work left to do in this world.

Perhaps, they may hear a voice calling for them from behind. As they are about to follow the spirits crossing over the river, they may hear a voice from behind, and the moment they turn around, they find themselves back in this earthly world. Or, some return to this world thanks to doctors who are a little aggressive. Just as they start to cross the river, a doctor may come in right on time to give them good, hard slaps on the cheek and tell them, "Don't give up! You can't die now. Come back!" Some patients survive thanks to being slapped hard across the face.

When the patients' souls return to their physical bodies, they will suddenly feel acute pain and regret that they have come back. In this way, some people come back to this world without crossing over the River Styx. This is because they have a mission to tell others about what they experienced in the other world. Others come back because they still have remaining work to accomplish in this world, and it is not yet their time to return to the other world.

On the other hand, there are also cases when people end their lives much earlier than originally planned because their physical bodies cannot be sustained. For instance, when the body suffers heavy damage due to an accident, the soul cannot return to it, no matter how hard it tries. If a bomb drops close by during war, there will be no physical body for the soul to return to in the first place. There is no way back in these kinds of situations. A person may have the chance to come back to life, but once their soul crosses the River Styx, the decision is final. The soul will be guided by the spirits in heaven to enter the next world.

4
Guidance in the Other World

Spirits of the deceased will be guided based on their religious faith

In most cases, spirits of religious figures will guide the deceased in the other world. Many people in this world belong to a particular religion, such as Japanese Shinto, Buddhism, and Christianity, and indeed, it is better to belong to one. If people do not belong to any religion, spirits in the Spirit World will have difficulty guiding them after death because they do not know who to send for help. So, it is good that there are different religious groups in this world. If you do not belong to a particular religion, spirits in the other world will argue over who will go and help you when you die, but if you belong to one, spirits of that religion will take charge of looking after you. You will be guided smoothly after that.

If you are a Christian, for example, a Christian angel will come to guide you, and you will head to a church after you cross the River Styx. There are churches in the other world where the spirits who have just arrived will go. There, the guiding and guardian angels gather the newcomers and give sermons, explain various things about life in the Spirit World, and teach them to reflect on their lives in this world. There is one-on-one guidance as well. A guiding angel will tell you, "Let's review your life," and you will recall the events from your life in this world. In the past, many spirits did not understand when they were told to "rewind their life and review it," but now that videotapes are more common, they have a better idea.

If you are a Buddhist, you will go to a Buddhist temple. Temples and shrines exist in the other world as well. In this way, spirits who have just returned to the other world are gathered at a religious facility based on the religious faith they had while they were alive, and they will receive guidance about the other world.

"El Cantare Cathedral" in the other world

Buildings in the other world are far more magnificent than the ones you see in this world. Many Christians who had a near-death experience reported that they saw a cathedral made of clear quartz crystals. It is impossible to build a cathedral like that in this world. In reality, it is most probably crystals of light, but many have reported visiting a cathedral made of quartz crystals. It seems that Christian buildings appear like that in the other world. Buddhist buildings are also beautiful. So as not to be outdone by Christian churches, their temple roofs are made with gold, for example. Various things are done on the Buddhist side as well to make their temples more magnificent than those found in this world.

Happy Science is currently building shojas (temples) in many places around the world, and our temples are taking shape in the other world as well. We have lots of believers all across Japan, which means there will be many Happy Science believers who pass away each year. These people need a place where they can gather after leaving this world, which is why we are building the "El Cantare Cathedral" in the other world. It is a breathtaking and magnificent building. The stairs leading to the entrance gate are made of marble, and the interior of the cathedral is made of refined and clear jewels and crystals, not concrete. The altar is made of gold and diamonds, and the dome ceiling is transparent, allowing light to shine through. It is an exquisite religious building.

Each region in this world has its own spirit realm and also its own local River Styx. Spirits of the deceased cross the River Styx of their own region, so it is very difficult to gather all of them in one place. This is why there is an urgent need to build more of our temples in the Spirit

World, especially in regions where there are many Happy Science believers. It is not easy for the spirits who have just died to travel dozens or hundreds of miles to get together in one place. It would be surprising if they could quickly get a hold of things in the Spirit World; usually, they are clueless as to what is happening around them.

Currently, Happy Science is building temples all over the world, and soon, they will appear in many areas of the Spirit World as well. They will be more beautiful and more glorious than the ones in this world. Unless we build our own temples in the other world, our believers will be confused about where to go. When they return to the other world, they might be baffled, thinking, "The Buddhist temple is not where I belong, and the church doesn't fit me either because I'm not a Christian. The Shinto shrine with the *torii* gate is not exactly my place either." Passionate Happy Science believers will not be satisfied with other religious facilities, so we need to put up an RO sign (the symbol of Happy Science) or a billboard that says, "We recite 'The True Words Spoken By Buddha' (the fundamental sutra of Happy Science)," outside our temples in the other world.

The importance of spreading the names of "Ryuho Okawa" and "Happy Science"

Happy Science lecturers and believers who are passionately doing missionary work will take on the work of guiding others after they die and return to the other world. Of course, they will first need to study more about the other world, but after a certain period of studying, they will begin to provide guidance about the Spirit World to the spirits who have recently returned there and have no idea where they are. These lecturers and believers will work as so-called "guiding angels" and preach to the newcomers at churches, shrines, and temples in the other world. They may consult newcomers individually and teach them where they went wrong during their lives in this world, or how they should live as spirits from now on. Most believers of Happy Science will probably take on this work. You cannot become a bodhisattva without doing this work and accumulating enough experience. If our lecturers and believers do not take on this work, I would be extremely busy even after returning to the other world.

According to the accounts of near-death experiences, Jesus often appeared before Christian believers, but it is questionable whether who they saw was really Jesus. Considering the number of Christians in the world, I assume that tens of thousands of them pass away each day, so if Jesus were to appear before every single one of them, he would be extremely busy. Thus, there is no doubt that Jesus' disciples are the ones going around guiding them. At that time, his disciples try to appear like Jesus, with reddish blonde hair, a slim body, sandals, and a white robe. His disciples are working hard to look like Jesus so they can guide the spirits.

When the soul of a great Christian angel who was born as a human passes away, perhaps Jesus will go and see them himself, but if he visited every Christian who died in a car accident or for other reasons, it would be too taxing. He would not even have enough time to contemplate. He would end up being like a blue-collar worker. Perhaps, Jesus himself may go visit important people when they die, but that is probably limited to a few times a day. Usually, his disciples handle this work, as Jesus also needs to study various things and has other duties to fulfill. I am sure that it is Jesus' line of disciples, such as angels and angels-to-be, who are wearing religious clothing and guiding the spirits of Christians who have died. This explains why so many Christians who have had a near-death experience report having seen Jesus Christ after seeing their own deceased family relatives. Some even say that they saw God. This is probably because the spirits are so bright that they take them for God.

In the Christian history of two thousand years, there have been hundreds of saints and other famous figures, but not all of them are well-known. These figures will not be recognized even if they introduce themselves. Nonetheless, everyone knows of Jesus. That is why many Christian angels disguise themselves as Jesus and act like him to guide the spirits. There are many guardian angels in Christianity. If they introduce themselves and are told, "I don't know who you are," they will be disheartened. They will be upset, so they rarely reveal their names; you would need to be Jesus or at least one of the seven archangels to be able to reveal your name and be recognized. That is why it is also important to be well-known.

It is difficult to save spirits when they do not recognize who has come to guide them. In a way, to be well-known is closely related to the power to save people. Even famous figures like Mother Teresa and Albert Schweitzer are not known to everyone. If a spirit does not know Mother Teresa or Albert Schweitzer, who has come to save them, the spirit will only say, "I don't know you," and will not listen to what they have to say. Then, they will have no choice but to pass the baton to other angels that the spirit knows.

It is often said that public relations (PR) began with religion. Indeed, PR is essential. It is important for many people to know the names "Ryuho Okawa" and "Happy Science." Saving the spirits in the other world becomes very difficult if they simply tell you, "What's Happy Science?" So, it is very important to make Happy Science well-known and even more important to have people believe in its teachings. Then, the spirits will be guided much more smoothly in the other world.

The importance of being connected to a religion

It is better to be connected to some kind of religion, even if you are not deeply involved with it. If you have no connection to religion at all, you will have a hard time after you die. Usually, when people die, their father, mother, or other relatives are likely to come to see them, but this is not always the case. Sometimes, their relatives cannot come because they are in the middle of their own spiritual training. In such cases, the spirit that just arrived in the other world will not be able to receive prompt help, and it may struggle with what to do. For this reason, it is better to have some kind of connection to a religion.

Even if you, yourself, do not believe in God, you can still be connected to religion through someone who believes in God, such as your friend. This is something to be grateful for. For example, when people with faith have a nonreligious friend who passed away, they will be worried about what will happen to the friend in the other world. So they will sincerely pay tribute or pray that the friend will return to heaven smoothly. Thanks to their prayers, their deceased friend will be connected with their guardian spirits or the spirit group of their religion. Then, arrangements will be made, and their friend will know where to go.

If you have no guidance at all, things will be tough after you return to the other world. After death, your soul will leave your physical body, travel through a tunnel into a world of light, and walk across the flower field until you reach the River Styx. In Japan, the border between this world and the other world usually takes the form of a river, but it may look like a lake to some. In Switzerland, the souls will climb over a mountain instead of crossing the River Styx. The souls of the deceased will experience various things, so they need someone to guide them. For this reason, religious people spread the Truth in this world to guide others, and if they could not guide others sufficiently while alive, they will continue to guide the spirits in the other world as well. I would like you to know that.

There are countless spirits in the other world who are working to guide the spirits of the deceased. If you witness the work that they are doing, you will realize that each person is truly cherished. There are billions of people on earth, and every day, someone dies in an accident or of illness. All of this information is immediately transmitted to the Spirit World, and the spirits with a connection to the deceased will come to guide them. Not only their friends and relatives but also those of religious professions, who have already returned to the other world, will come to help them. This is a blessing. Lots of spirits in the other world know when a person dies. This makes me realize how truly cherished each person is. I am sure many of you will eventually take on this work of guiding others.

5
Recollecting and Reflecting on Your Life

Looking at yourself from a third-person perspective

When you die, you will recollect your life on earth in a series of flashbacks. This recollection takes place differently from person to person. Some will see their lives reflected in a Life-Reflecting Mirror, while others will see it as if on a movie screen. There are yet others who will see snapshots of various scenes of their lives, one after another.

According to the reports of a near-death experience, surprisingly, everyone said that there was no such thing as time in the other world. The concept of time does not exist in the other world because it comes from the Earth's rotation. Everyone who has had a near-death experience testified that there was no time or space in the other world, and they are, indeed, right. After you die, you will recall your entire, several decade long life in just an instant, so you will be surprised and think, "How is this possible?" Normally, it should at least take a few years to watch even the digest version of your life. But in reality, every detail of your life will be recalled in a matter of a split second, including various events that took place in your childhood.

It is said that you will recall everything—both good and bad memories. You will recall, for example, a time when you got into a fight with others or when you succeeded in doing something. You will also remember your relationship with your parents, siblings, your own children, and friends, as well as your times at school, and your experiences of job hunting. At that time, you will not only look at your life from your own perspective; interestingly enough, you will see it from a third-person perspective. Suppose you had picked a fight with your friend during your childhood. You would watch that scene from someone else's eyes, which means that it is not a scene from your own memory. In fact, this information is provided by your guardian spirit. The "videotape" of your life records the images you saw and the impressions you had, and it also contains the images recorded by your guardian spirit. That is why you can look at yourself from a third-person perspective.

What is more, when you are looking at your past self, it feels like you are there in real time, as if you have traveled back a few decades in a time machine. But although you are there, people around you cannot see you. You may see, for instance, a scene where you are bullying your friend as a child, just like the character "Gian (Big G)" from the Japanese anime *Doraemon*. You will certainly recall having bullied your friend, but you will also feel what the bullied friend was feeling at that time. You will understand what is running through the mind of your friend: the pain of getting beaten up, sadness, and a sense of betrayal that comes with it. You will also feel your friend worrying about how to explain to their mom and dad when they get home, or whether they can go to school the next day. All their worries and suffering will flow into your heart. You probably remember that you had bullied someone, but not only will you recall that memory, you will also understand the feelings of the person you bullied. This allows you to look at your past objectively and fairly. You will look at various events of your life like this, one by one.

Experiencing another person's life for yourself

Let us say that you remember finding success at work, such as closing a big deal or beating out another company. You will certainly see these events when you recollect the memories of your life, but at that time, you will also see what happened afterwards to the person on the losing end. You may, for example, see your competitor going home discouraged after losing against you, being demoted or laid off shortly after, and end up working at a small food stall selling *oden* (Japanese hot-pot dish) a year later. You would not know what happened to your opponent after the competition, as you did not see them afterward, but those things will be shown to you in the other world. You will discover what kind of situations your opponent went through after losing to you, such as getting into a dispute with his wife that led to a tragic ending, or driving their children to become delinquent.

In the other world, you will see what happened to others as a result of your actions or your involvement. Some of you will see this as if watching a video, while others will relive it vividly as if they are there in real time. At that time, you may try to talk to the people there, but they will not hear you. You may explain to the person you hurt that you did not mean to put them in misery, but the person will not hear you.

According to multiple accounts of near-death experience, a person who worked as a weapon dealer saw what happened as a result of doing his job. He, himself, only remembered selling weapons, but he was also shown how the weapons were used afterward, how people died from them, and how the victims' families went through deep sorrow and a hard life after that. Some weapon dealers even relived the pain of the victims' families, crying over the dead body and having a funeral.

In the earthly sense, weapon dealers are simply selling weapons. They are indifferent to what happens after that, such as how those weapons are used and who dies from them. But all of those subsequent events are recorded in the Spirit World. For this reason, you can say that those who dropped the atomic bombs on Hiroshima and Nagasaki must have suffered tremendously after they died. They may have just obeyed their superior's orders, but no matter how hard they tried to justify themselves, reliving the agony and suffering of the victims and their bereaved families must have been tremendously painful for them.

Once you move on to the Spirit World, you will experience these things. When you look at your life in a series of flashbacks in the other world, it looks different from how you remember it, as you will see your life's events from a third-person perspective and understand the feelings of the other person involved. You will also be shown how your actions affected the lives of others. You may have had various experiences with others, such as falling out with someone, or dating and breaking up with a partner. In the other world, you will be shown what happened to these people after they parted from you. Shortly after you die, you will learn these things in the other world. Your destination in the Spirit World will not be determined until you have reviewed and reflected on your entire life in this way.

As you are shown each scene from your life, you will be asked, "What do you think of this scene? Do you think you did the right thing? What do you think you should have done at that time?"

Perhaps you brought flowers for your sick colleague at the hospital. But if it was just for show and you were really thinking, "Serves you right! Thank God, I have one less rival to deal with," those thoughts will also be exposed. In the world after death, your life will be shown as though you are experiencing it in real time, as if you are watching a drama.

6
The Spirit World Cannot Be Proved Logically

Past, present, and future coexist in the Spirit World

When you recall your life in this world in the other world, you will realize that the concept of time in the Spirit World is completely different from that in the earthly world; you will feel as if you have stepped into the scenes of the past. This is what I mean when I say that in the Spirit World, the concept of time—the past, present, and future—seems to exist but does not at the same time. What happened in the past will seem like it is happening in the present. So, you can experience past events as if you have jumped into a movie, which is, in effect, the same as time-traveling to the past.

To tell the truth, what happens in the future is also revealed to certain spirits. They witness future events as if they are taking place in the present. They can experience how the future world will unfold if things continue the way they are now. At the same time, they also learn that a future event can be changed, although it seems like it has already happened. This is indeed a mysterious experience. In the *Back to the Future* movie series, there is a story about how the protagonist's future could have been changed if his parents had not gotten married at a particular point in the past. The future changed depending on what occurred at each turning point in life. There are scenes where the inscribed name on a tombstone or the images in a photo kept appearing differently. In the same way, the future can actually change.

In a way, the future is set, but at the same time, it can also be changed. The future—in the sense of how things will turn out if things continue the way they are now—is set and has already occurred in the Spirit World, so you can experience that version of the future. However, it is still possible to change it. The Spirit World is such a mysterious world. Therefore, in the Spirit World, the past, present, and future do not exist in the same way as we measure time with a clock in this world. Rather, the past, present, and future co-exist in the same space. Nevertheless, there is a set order of "which comes first and which comes later," and this sequence will not change, just like how the parents always come before the child. This is the Spirit World.

The law of cause and effect is the only logic in the other world

People who have received a science-based education often say that they do not believe in things that cannot be proved scientifically or explained logically. In the other world, however, things do not occur according to worldly logic. The Spirit World is not a logical world. So, it is impossible to logically explain the world that is not logical. Trying to do so is the same as attempting to measure the size of the sky with a 12-inch ruler, as I said at the beginning of this chapter.

The only logic that you could say exists in the Spirit World is the law of cause and effect, which is taught at Happy Science. It is the law of *cause*, *condition*, *effect*, and *reward*. There is a cause for everything, and when certain conditions are met, it produces an effect, which then invites a reward. This logical order of cause, condition, effect, and reward exists in the other world. This kind of causal relationship certainly exists, but nothing else is logical in the other world.

To explain it more easily, the Spirit World is similar to the world of radio waves, such as television and radio. In terms of books, it is more similar to the world of fiction, like novels, rather than academic books. All kinds of events can happen in a novel, and anything is possible. The Spirit World is very akin to this. A novel is not written logically. The characters intertwine with each other in many ways, and various dramas unfold randomly. This is very similar to the way things happen in the Spirit World. The other world is not logical, and it does feel unrealistic in a way. Things you never imagined could happen can occur. It is a world where anything can happen, completely irrelevant to time and space. In the Spirit World, knowing is power. If you know something, you can make it happen.

In the Spirit World, you will sometimes see things in a symbolic way rather than in a realistic way. In other words, some things will appear as a symbol rather than in their original form, and you will have to figure out what they mean. What you will see cannot be logically explained; it is similar to fantasy or illusion. So, in some cases, spirits may be looking at the same thing but perceiving it differently. The world they witness is different depending on their level of understanding.

What does it mean to see something in a symbolic way? I mentioned that people who had a near-death experience have reported seeing a flower field, but this is just a symbol. A flower field likely symbolizes a beautiful world. People have also seen many beautiful, jewel-like pebbles at the bottom of a river and various other sceneries. These, too, symbolize different things. It is difficult to explain the other world in words, but basically, you can understand it as being similar to the imaginative pictures that children draw. The Spirit World is similar to the world where the pictures you have drawn from imagination have become a reality. In that sense, the other world is close to the world of magic.

Some people have experienced this unique sense of the Spirit World and come back to this world. These people will be stunned when they hear others say, "I don't believe in things that cannot be explained in a scientific way." To them, what these "scientific" people are saying sounds absurd and nonsensical. It is as if they are in a 25-meter pool filled with thick gelatin and yet insisting that they will measure or do something with the nail that they found at the bottom of the pool.

This is actually what I feel when I look at modern medicine. They place too much emphasis on the brain and try to explain everything as a result of the brain's function. They even try to explain the human soul in connection with brain function. They say, for example, that a near-death experience is simply caused by brain activity. According to their hypothesis, the brain releases morphine in the moments before death, which makes the patient feel a sense of bliss. In reality, however, according to spirits, both the flower field and the River Styx will unfold before the patient's eyes even after they die and their physical body has been cremated. Therefore, the near-death experience has nothing to do with the brain's morphine secretion.

7
People Who Fall to Hell

Your level of enlightenment determines your destination in the afterlife

I mentioned how the soul passes through a tunnel to enter the world of light during a near-death experience. This is what ordinary people will experience after they die: those who have little knowledge or experience of the afterlife and have lived every day influenced by the three-dimensional, earthly vibrations. In my case, I will head straight into the Spirit World without going through the tunnel.

Currently, I exist in the third dimensional world. However, in reality, all other dimensional spaces—fourth, fifth, sixth, seventh, eighth, and ninth dimensions—coexist within the space of this third dimension. Shakyamuni Buddha taught that the level of enlightenment you have attained in this world corresponds to the dimension you will return to in the other world, and this is, indeed, correct. Your destination in the other world is determined by how well you can control your mind and which dimensional level of enlightenment you have attained.

People who have little control over their minds are constantly emitting third-dimensional, earthly vibrations, so they will struggle a lot to make the transition into the fourth dimension after they die. They need to remove their earthly vibrations, as if physically shedding their skin or shell. Even after they return to the other world, they need to wash away the great deal of dirt they picked up in this world. First, they will cleanse the dirt of their minds that they accumulated from various experiences of this world, then explore the true nature of time and space, and then learn the true nature of human beings. Only after they have learned all these things can they finally understand the purpose and mission of their lives. They will at least realize and say, "So, that was the purpose of my life!"

Having families, such as your parents, children, and siblings, is also something to be thankful for. When you go to the other world, your close family members who have already passed away will definitely come to welcome you, so having a family is indeed a blessing. Others will rarely come to see you unless they have a close relationship with you.

People who fall headfirst into hell

Most reports of a near-death experience are about going to a world of peace, but there are other cases, too. I guess people would not want to share their experience if it is not a peaceful one. There must be quite a lot of people in this modern age who have experienced going to hell.

In the worst-case scenario, people will fall straight to hell; they literally feel themselves falling headfirst into it. This is a subjective feeling, but it feels like they are falling deep down until they hit the center of the Earth. It feels like they are in a free-falling elevator, or they jumped into a bottomless well and are falling from an incredible height of tens or hundreds of miles. They cannot even work out how long or how far they are falling. Eventually, they will land somewhere, but it is completely dark, just like the break of dawn, and they have to grope their way through the dark. As they remain alone in the cold for a while, they will gradually see their surroundings. What they see next is similar to the world of hell depicted in the Happy Science movies, such as *Hermes—Winds of Love* and *The Laws of the Sun* (Executive Producer Ryuho Okawa).

Some will find themselves in a dark place like that, while others will land in a volcanic area where lava is bubbling, or fire is shooting up. Perhaps, some may be assaulted as soon as they land somewhere. I am sure that some of you have had nightmares where you were chased by someone with a sword, a bat, or a machine gun, when you were suffering from a high fever, for example. In the same way, some will go through a terrifying experience shortly after having fallen into the dark abyss, such as being chased by those who are trying to harm them. These experiences will feel very real. People who have lived their lives always believing that someone is out to get them will most likely end up in hell and undergo these kinds of frightening experiences.

The world of hell is expansive and limitless. All kinds of events are unfolding in this world.

People who walk down to hell

Nowadays, many people die in a hospital, so in most cases, souls will leave their physical bodies that are lying on the hospital bed, move through the tunnel, cross the River Styx, and then enter the other world. After that, they will go to a church or temple and reflect on their lives. Then, their destinations in the other world will finally be determined.

As a result of self-reflection, some will decide to stay in the fourth dimensional Astral Realm to undergo further spiritual training, while others will choose to go to hell. In the latter case, you will write down your repentance, saying, "My life didn't reach a passing grade. I regret that I lived the wrong way." You will then talk with your guardian spirit about how long you should undergo spiritual training in hell, and then head to hell on your own accord.

You will be told what kind of spiritual training you need to undergo in hell to redeem the karma you accumulated during your life, and then be guided in the direction you should head toward. As you walk in that direction, you will see a downward slope beyond the gentle hill with beautiful flowers, and you will understand that you have to follow that slope. There are several paths to take, but these paths all slope downward. As you go down one of those paths, you will notice the surrounding scenery gradually changing from a beautiful flower field to a rocky terrain, just like the lava beds of Mt. Asama and Mt. Aso. Trees become shorter like shrubs and are sparsely scattered. Gradually, the sky turns cloudy and darker, and the temperature falls.

You will go on a short journey like this, and along the way, you will have various experiences. There are many things at the border of hell, and you will meet various spirits. Many are lost and wandering around in the area. There are also spirits who are trying to trick others, and those who are guiding the way for others. There are yet others who are coming up the slope. Some of them may greet you and say, "I've finally managed to come back. Are you heading there now? Hang in there. Even hell will grow on you as you spend a long time there. Once your spiritual training is over, you'll realize that all was for the best. I went through 60 years of spiritual training, and I'm now headed back up." You may also hear others saying, "Oh, I see my dear guardian spirit coming to guide me." Sometimes, you will pass by these spirits and feel envious that they have finished their spiritual training.

Nevertheless, those who go down to hell in this manner did not commit heavy sins. They are conscious of their sins, which means that they are not as bad as those who fall headfirst into hell.

People who are taken to hell by the devil

In the case of people who were possessed by a number of evil spirits or devils while alive, their souls will most likely be taken to hell straightaway by these spirits, as if being abducted. Unfortunately, they will not be greeted by their deceased grandparents or angels, or go through the tunnel into the world of light. This is because they had already become devils' minions while they were alive, and were working to fulfill their evil mission. They were part of the "special force" dispatched to this world by devils and were fulfilling their role as the devils' tools. The souls of these people will end up going straight to hell.

They are, for instance, mafia-like individuals, drug dealers who ruined other people's lives, frauds, robbers, criminals, and leaders who killed many people. When such people who acted as devils' minions die, their fellow minions of the devil will come along and take them away immediately. In this case, even angels cannot help them because they are in tune with devils. Evil spirits will take them away like in a rugby scrum, leaving no room for the angels to even speak to them. The only way to save the souls of these people is to have them experience hell until they have had enough of it, just as it is said in the Zen proverb, "One must experience hot and cold for oneself."

I have given a general description of the world of hell. In contrast, the higher worlds of the Spirit World are wonderful places, as I have described in other books.

8
The Other World Is Governed by Religion

Many people in this world are living without knowing the Truth

The spirit of the late writer T. K., who was a member of Happy Science, sometimes comes to visit me. One day, he told me this: "It has been several years since I returned to the other world, and everything I have experienced here is exactly as you have said, Master. Everything is just the way you have taught us, without a single thing amiss. Nevertheless, most people in this world live and die without ever knowing the Truth. These people will be in serious trouble when they come to the other world. I think that Happy Science needs to put more effort into missionary work. I don't think it's enough at the moment. There are billions of people in this world, so our members shouldn't be satisfied with just making your books multi-million-selling bestsellers. A few million people may have read your books, but that is still not enough; the Truth has not reached everyone. Most people fall through the net of salvation. The other world is exactly as you have described it, so we must let more people know of this Truth."

I told him that we should not rush too much, as this world has its own rules and things do not go so easily. But those who really know the Truth usually insist that we must let everyone know the Truth as quickly as possible. They say that it is too unkind to leave more than half the population clueless about the Truth.

The world after death is not a place of suffering or sadness. Of course, it is for those who lived in the wrong way, but for those who lived righteously, the other world is a far more beautiful, peaceful, and happier place than this earthly world. It is so wonderful that virtually no one who has experienced it wants to come back to this world.

In fact, life in this world is a kind of test. For a certain period of time, people accumulate various experiences in this world and are being tested on how they live while having their eyes covered to the Truth. Depending on the results of this test, the world of suffering may be waiting for them after death. For this reason, not knowing the Truth is a serious problem. In this modern society, many people consider the Truth as an unscientific superstition or an outdated idea that archaic people believed in. A society like this is dangerous.

Today, many people do not believe in the world after death, and this has brought confusion to the other world. The world population is currently increasing, and there seem to be many souls who were born into this world for the first time. Among them are souls that are not originally humans but formerly living creatures that lived closely with humans. What is more, many souls from outer space have come to Earth, and some of them live here in a physical body for the very first time. That is why things have become quite chaotic. So, I would like everyone to know and believe in the other world while they are still alive, and after returning to the other world, experience and confirm the truth for themselves.

In the other world, you cannot live without religion

We, Happy Science believers, must carry out the work of salvation in this world. This work will continue even after we die and return to the other world.

When you die and return to the other world, you will realize how important religion truly is. Although religion is often despised or ridiculed in this earthly world, it is highly respected in the other world. The other world is mostly governed by religion. There, you cannot live without religion because without it, you cannot exist. Some Happy Science believers may be undergoing their soul training as they persevere in poverty, but these people will be met with a beautiful, dazzling world once they return to the other world. This world may be filled with sufferings, difficulties, or persecution, but in the other world, religion is in the majority. Everything is based on religion.

People may refuse to believe in religion, the afterlife, spirits, angels, and Buddha or God, but they will either become earth-bound spirits and cling to people in this world, their companies, houses, or tombstones, or they will fall straight into the Abysmal Hell, where ideological criminals who led many people astray gather. What is more, some spirits in hell have "faith," that is, faith in devils, to be exact. There are those who believe in the wrong teachings, so simply having faith is not enough. There are parts of hell that are under the control of misguided religions. Even so, over 95 percent of the other world is governed by righteous religions. In this sense, the work of religion is immensely important.

Self-reflection and prayer are "cell phones" that allow you to connect to the higher Spirit World

In this world, religion does not have enough power to fight, and there are not enough people who take on religious work. That is why we are struggling to convince people to believe in the Truth. As I mentioned earlier, people are coming up to us saying, "Prove it to me with this 12-inch ruler," but we are still unable to refute them. This is the current situation.

Ultimately, everyone will experience the Spirit World after they die. But the problem is that scientism, based on materialism, is driving modern people into the depths of delusion and the world of ignorance. We must do everything we can to save these people from falling into such a world. As I said in the episode with the late writer T. K., we should not be satisfied with just making million-sellers. He is right about that. Millions is too small a number compared to Earth's population. It is also questionable how many people who have read my books truly understand my teachings.

I also mentioned that people will recollect their lives after death, but in the case of Happy Science believers, they are already doing that while they are still alive. They self-reflect and meditate by recollecting past events during their practice of self-reflection. Without taking a quiet time to reflect on yourself, you can never be able to communicate with other dimensional worlds.

If any of you, by chance, end up in a dark world after death, please use prayer. Prayer is like a phone call; your thoughts will definitely reach the other side. You could end up living in the wrong way and fail to return to the world of light, although you may have believed that you practiced self-reflection and underwent spiritual training. At such times, please pray. Your prayer will definitely reach heaven, and some kind of salvation will come down to you. An angel may come to save you, or other means of help will be given to you.

Do not forget to pray. Even a short prayer is effective.

I want as many people as possible to not only become avid readers of my books but also become the believers of Happy Science. At the same time, I would like them to gain the knowledge of the Spirit World, practice self-reflection properly while they are still alive, and pray and practice meditation in our temples and shojas. These practices will become the tools that allow you to contact the higher Spirit World. It is important to have these tools. Self-reflection, prayer, and the recitation of Happy Science sutras are "cell phones" that allow you to connect to the higher dimensional world of the Spirit World. I would like as many people as possible to experience making these phone calls.

When you look at the Real World or the other world, you will realize that there is still a lot of remaining work you have to do in this world. The current state shows how difficult it is to live in this world. So, I strongly wish to spread the teachings and activities of Happy Science far and wide.

CHAPTER THREE

What Is Faith?

—Question and Answer Sessions

1
Why Does God Exist?

[Question]
This is the question I've asked myself since I was a child. Why does God exist?

The Fourth Public Lecture held on July 8, 1989
at Sonic City in Saitama, Japan.

There is something that runs through everyone's heart

All human beings carry the mark of being created. We can breathe oxygen as soon as we are born as babies. We have a mouth, eyes, a nose, and ears. Our physical bodies are perfectly designed for living in this world. This is actually too good to be true and an incredible thing. If you study Happy Science teachings, you will also learn about the soul. The deeper you study the soul, the more you will understand just how valuable it is. If you contemplate what lies at the basis of this value, you will come to assume that humans are indeed created beings.

Everyone feels or thinks differently. Even so, everyone is moved without exception when they hear words that touch their heart. Not all people have common ancestors or are related, yet they are all moved when they hear heart-touching words. Even if they are from different countries, their souls will be shaken in the same way when they come across words of Truth that are translated properly. In this respect, everyone is the same.

Why is this? It is because people have the ability to understand one another even if they are separate individuals. The reason they can understand each other is that they all share the same feelings within themselves. You will not understand feelings that you do not possess. It is precisely because you share the same senses or feelings as others that you can understand them. All kinds of people are living in different environments; there are people you have never met, people on the other side of the globe, people across Africa, and people from India, for example. Regardless, everyone shares something in common that flows in their heart.

In this earthly world, each person is born from their own parents, but ultimately, they are all connected to each other through their heart and soul. Billions of people are now living in this world, but they are all connected to one another. Despite the difference in their patterns of behavior, the languages they speak, or the colors of their hair or skin, they certainly have something in common at the depths of their hearts, in their sense of values, in their moral code, and in the Truth they believe in. If we explore what lies at the source of all this, we will find the existence of the Being we call God or Buddha. Thus, we can assume that the soul was created by God.

Looking at what is inside people's minds, we cannot help but feel the existence of God. Let us take America and Africa, for example. Many different races of people live there, and they all have a conscience. Why is that? Why are they all able to understand what is right? Why are they all able to find something to be beautiful? Although there are slight differences in what they consider right or beautiful since they come from different environments, they generally understand these concepts in the same way. They all have a conscience, and their hearts ache when they do something wrong.

This is not only true with humans but also with dogs and cats. If you have a dog at home, you may notice that, when it does something wrong, it looks down and puts on a sad face as if it is aware of what it did. The same is true with cats. Not only humans but animals also have a kind of conscience. Why is that? Although animals have a body and soul that are completely different from those of humans, they, too, can understand some degree of right and wrong. I believe that this shows that all living beings are branched off from the same Origin.

The Parent of souls undeniably exists

Now, let me ask you a question: "Why do you have parents?" Can you answer it? You would probably say, "I don't know, but if it weren't for my parents, I wouldn't be here." In the same way, humans cannot answer the question, "Why does God exist?" This is because humans are in no position to question God. What is clear is that, as children of God, humans must admit that the Parent of souls exists.

No one has ever successfully proved the existence of our Parent in this earthly world, but a number of people have continued to provide evidence that leads us to draw that conclusion. I, too, have been providing different kinds of evidence to successfully prove the existence of our Parent. Ultimately, it is up to each and every person's heart to decide whether they acknowledge the existence of the Parent. I cannot force you into acknowledging Him. But I have so far published over 400 books (3,250 books as of 2026) and given many lectures to offer you various opportunities to find the Truth. So I would like you to take this fact into account to decide for yourself.

As long as we are humans, it is impossible to define God and explain everything about Him. However, it is possible for humans to guess or assume the existence of this Being and talk about Him.

2
The Significance of Belonging to a Religious Organization

[Question]
I have heard of a phrase, "Don't follow people or religious groups, but follow the Dharma or the teachings." If we were to adhere to this phrase, it would mean that we should not belong to a religious group. Please tell us the significance of becoming a believer of a religious organization.

The Eighth Public Lecture held on July 29, 1990
at Aichi Prefectural Gymnasium in Aichi, Japan.

People who study the Truth alone tend to become self-satisfied

The idea you raised will lead you to be a self-styled practitioner or become self-satisfied. A self-styled practitioner simply enjoys the feeling of being enlightened; in other words, their enlightenment is not yet real. If you are interpreting "Don't follow people or religious groups, but follow the Dharma" as "staying away from a religious organization," you have yet to attain real enlightenment. You do not understand the true meaning of this phrase. People who read books and study on their own tend to interpret things in a way that is most convenient to them.

The true meaning of the phrase, "Don't follow people or organizations, but follow the Dharma," is as follows: "When there is someone preaching the Dharma, follow the Dharma that he is preaching. When the person preaching the Dharma passes away, follow the teachings that he has left behind." This is a Buddhist teaching called "The Inner Torch and the Torch of Dharma." From long ago, Buddhism has taught, "While Buddha is alive, follow Buddha's teachings. After Buddha is gone, follow the Dharma he has left behind; each person must live by lighting the torch within their own mind."

While it is easy to interpret words literally, people often misunderstand the real meaning behind them. If you have an earnest desire to seek and explore the teachings, you should learn from a proper master. There are some things you will not understand unless you are taught by a master.

Devote yourself to the Three Treasures of Buddha, Dharma, and Sangha

It is important to devote yourself to the Three Treasures of Buddha, Dharma, and Sangha. Buddha means the enlightened one, Dharma means the teachings spoken by Buddha, and Sangha means the group of Buddha's disciples and the rules they should follow.

Once you become a believer and join the Sangha, your Dharma friends will teach you what you do not know. But some people reject help from others and say that they can attain enlightenment on their own. These people can attain the enlightenment of "solitary realizers" (those who awaken and enlighten on their own, without a master), but their enlightenment will not go beyond a certain level. Ultimately, it is better to become a believer and join the Sangha, and learn the Truth under a master, together with Dharma friends.

3
The Developmental Stages of Faith

[Question]
Are there also developmental stages to faith?

The Third Special Public Lecture held on November 23, 1990
at Okinawa Convention Center in Okinawa, Japan.

Faith has an infinite number of stages

In my book, *The Laws of the Sun* (New York: IRH Press, 2018), I have described the developmental stages of love, which are fundamental love, nurturing love, forgiving love, and love incarnate. Now that you ask me whether there are developmental stages to faith in God, I will answer, "Yes, of course." In fact, there are almost an infinite number of developmental stages to faith. Faith is actually a staircase that leads to the Ultimate God. If you ask me how many different levels of faith there are, I must say that there are thousands, tens of thousands, or even more. To be honest, there are almost infinite stages of faith.

On hearing this, some people may become disheartened and think, "There is no way I can continue making efforts if there are almost an infinite number of stages." But the stage of faith actually corresponds to the stage of enlightenment. Let us say you are able to receive some kind of signal from your guardian spirit, and you feel that you are being guided by it as you act. This is the stage when your mind is directed toward God, and you are making the right effort, for most of the time. As long as you are making the right effort, heading in the right direction, and not having wrong thoughts, your guardian spirit is surely protecting you. This is the first stage of faith that religious practitioners should aspire to attain.

In this first stage, you can easily receive Light from heaven. For example, when you study the Truth or recite Happy Science's fundamental sutra, "The True Words Spoken By Buddha," a halo will be emitted around the back of your head. When you are talking with someone face to face, he or she will suddenly feel warmth in their heart or become cheerful, although they may have looked gloomy at first. This happens because heavenly Light enters them through you as you speak to them. This is very akin to the state of arhat, which is the first stage of enlightenment.

Guidance from heaven will come in proportion to the level of your faith

It is difficult for humans to measure the level of their faith. Usually, it is measured by God and high spirits in the other world. But when you are conveying the Truth to others, you may sometimes find miracles occurring to you. By observing the kinds of miracles happening to you, you can get an idea of how strong your faith is.

Many miraculous events will start to occur when you are doing missionary activities based on faith. So, examine how often they occur to you or what kinds of miracles are occurring. Then, you will be able to tell clearly how much you have raised the level of your faith and from which level of spiritual being you are receiving guidance. No miracles will occur to those without faith. However, people with faith will find good things happen to them unexpectedly; they may receive positive reactions from others and achieve good results, which they never believed could happen a year ago. When more and more miraculous events like that happen, you can be sure that you have started to receive a considerable amount of Light from your guardian and guiding spirits.

In fact, the quality and quantity of guidance from the other world will come in proportion to your developmental stage of faith. Your guardian spirit is more or less at the same level as your soul, so if you realize that something much more powerful than your guardian spirit or your own capability is at work, it means a guiding spirit is helping you. A guiding spirit has come to you, saying, "You have now engaged in work that is beyond your capability, so let me guide you as an expert in that field."

When you find yourself doing what you never thought you were capable of doing, it means you have reached one level higher. If you observe Happy Science lecturers, you can roughly tell how many people they can teach and guide. Lecturers with a higher level of faith have the power to enlighten others, that is to say, the power to convince and change the minds of many people. If this power is weak, you can only change the hearts of one or two people, but those with strong power are able to awaken tens or hundreds of people all at once.

When your faith is firmly established, you can draw power from the other world accordingly and produce correspondingly good results. What happens in the other world will be brought down to this world. Usually, events that occur in the other world rarely occur in the earthly world, but if this world and the other world become one through faith, the principle of the other world will work in this world as well. Faith has the power to make the

Real World and the Phenomenal World one and the same. Through faith, you can transcend the walls of dimensions. This is how you can understand faith. So, faith also has developmental stages, although they are not as clearly distinguished as the developmental stages of love.

4
How to Understand the Term *Buddha*

[Question]

Buddhist scriptures say that Buddha has been Buddha from the very beginning. On the other hand, they also say that you can become a buddha after a long period of spiritual discipline. How should we understand the term *Buddha*?

The Third Public Lecture held on May 28, 1989
at Kobe Port Island Hall in Hyogo, Japan.

Buddha appears in two forms

Buddha, in the sense of the Being who transcends human attributes, manifests in two forms. One is the Being who has been working from the very beginning of time as Buddha in His own form and fulfilling His role; the other are beings who have split off from the original Buddha, dwelled in human bodies, undergone eternal spiritual discipline, and almost fully regained the original nature. Buddha can manifest in these two ways.

To tell the truth, not all souls were created at exactly the same point in time. Various groups of souls were created at different times and in different sets of circumstances. What is more, not only were some of them created at different times, but also for different purposes.

Let me explain this further by looking at the differences in the time of creation. Suppose ten billion souls were created about two billion years ago. This group of souls undergoes spiritual discipline through numerous reincarnations. Then, about a billion years later, let us say another several billion souls were created. Among the earlier group of souls must be some who have made progress to a considerable level after having undergone repeated reincarnations over one billion years. These souls could appear as buddhas to the group of souls created later, as if they had been at a high level of enlightenment from the very beginning. This is the ultimate secret of the universe, so I cannot reveal too much about it, but I can at least say that in most cases, the older the soul, the more progress it has made and the greater soul it has become.

But it is also true that within each group of souls, some were created first for a specific purpose, which is to take on the role of teachers. Take, for example, Japanese universities with a history of only a little more than one century. Many of them have a system that allows their graduates to become assistants, then assistant professors, and finally, professors there. But when the very first university was created, Japan needed to invite teachers from abroad, as it did not have any teachers yet. In the same way, when souls were first created, it was also necessary to create souls that served as teachers. Then, eventually, souls who developed outstanding abilities through the process of education also became teachers. I hope you will understand the term *Buddha* through this metaphor.

5
The Relationship between Faith and Knowledge

[Question]

When I teach people about faith in God, I sometimes feel that knowledge gets in the way of their faith. What is the relationship between faith and knowledge? How can we make these two elements compatible? Please teach us.

Weekday Seminar held on June 28, 1989
at Social & Cultural Hall in Tokyo, Japan.

God is the Master and humans are His servants

In considering the relationship between God and humans, I must say that God is the Master and humans are His servants. Without this kind of humble mind, it would be impossible for humans to have faith in God in the first place, and there would be no room for religions to form in this world. There exists an absolute, transcendental Being called God, and humans live as they receive His mercy and return gratitude to God. So, humans have been servants since the beginning of time.

The idea of being a servant, or the awareness of being in the position to serve and assist, contains an important way of thinking that gives rise to faith. In fact, this idea nurtures humility, which then gives birth to the spirit of devotion and faith. So, being in the position to serve has a very significant meaning. On the contrary, humans become arrogant when they think that they are the masters of all creation. As they live at the mercy of their selfish desires, they often end up creating a world of hell.

Profound knowledge does not clash with faith

The same can be said of the relationship between faith and knowledge. Truly meaningful knowledge is not something you can get actively. Some people may think, "I am the master. If I acquire knowledge, all paths will open for me," but this is only true up to a certain level. Truly profound knowledge is called wisdom, which involves the real experience of interacting with sublime beings, such as becoming one with the universe or with God or Buddha. Unless you fully stand in the position of a servant or are in an extremely passive state, you will not receive this abundant wisdom.

In reality, faith and knowledge do not clash with one another. It is only the lower level of knowledge—limited knowledge that is only useful in this earthly world—that clashes with faith. Truly profound knowledge does not. The two will become one and the same; rather, knowledge will work to raise faith, and faith will work to raise knowledge.

Some nuns, priests, and Zen monks possess an extremely high level of intellect, even if they did not receive a higher education. What does this imply exactly? In truth, they have deep insight, sharp intuition, and unclouded vision to look at things from a broad and elevated perspective. This kind of profound wisdom is far superior to the knowledge that can be measured by worldly things like paperwork or written tests. It is deeply connected with faith. You cannot reach this level of profound wisdom through academic effort alone, unless you put in a tremendous amount of effort into gaining it. Most people cannot reach this level of wisdom through just academic studies.

Talent is used by virtue

If you find that knowledge gets in the way of someone's faith, you must first shatter their knowledge. To do so, you need to grasp the wisdom that lies beyond the worldly knowledge that they value so much. As you continue making efforts to grasp it, you will start to feel as though you are talking to a child. When you have gained real knowledge or true intellect, the other person will appear like a child to you; it will seem as though you and that person are a parent and a child, or a teacher and a pupil. Then, he or she will no longer be able to take a defiant attitude when you talk to them. Instead, they will wonder, "Why can this person understand things so deeply? How is it possible that this person can understand the true nature of myself, other people, and society? How did this person gain such insights or intuition?" They will feel like learning from you for the first time. At this time, you can teach them.

So, this is nothing but your own issue. When you are teaching faith to others, you may sometimes feel that their knowledge is keeping them from awakening to faith. In that case, please strive to accumulate within yourself wisdom that is at a higher level than their knowledge. Then, wisdom will flow from you to others, just like how water flows from upstream to downstream. It is the same as how water flows in a channel. If you stand at a lower position than others, your "water" will not flow toward them. They will not listen to you because they think they are better than you. They do not accept what you say because they are thinking, "I am more knowledgeable," "I have studied more," or "I am superior." So you should aim to "let the water flow naturally from high to low."

This is a matter of talent and virtue. Talent and virtue have a clear hierarchical relationship. Talent is meant to serve virtue. At times, you may see someone who does not seem very clever supported by many geniuses and great figures. That is because that person possesses virtue. Talent is used by virtue—this is the relationship between them.

Talent is closely related to knowledge. Intellectual people indeed have talent. You need virtue to move the hearts of talented people and to have them act in the way you want. Although it is difficult to explain virtue, you can say that it is the total power of spiritual enlightenments. When you have this power, talented people will gather around you, serve you, and listen to you. So, when you feel that talented people do not listen to your opinions, remind yourself that you still lack virtue. You need to undergo further spiritual discipline to accumulate virtue.

6
What Is Faith?

[Question]
Did faith come into existence after hell was formed, or did it exist even before that? Please teach us what faith is.

Special Seminar held on January 24, 1993
at Akashi City Community Hall in Hyogo, Japan.

To have faith means to be able to say, "I'm a child of God"

I have once said that "Faith is the confirmation of the fact," which is a little paradoxical and an odd way of putting it. What I really meant by it was as follows: "The Great Universe was created by the Primordial God. First, there was the Will of God that allowed humans and various other creatures to live. Through His Will, all sorts of living creatures were born. It is God who created the Great Universe, gave birth to various lives in it, and is nurturing them. These lives undergo soul training in many different ways in the Phenomenal World. As part of their soul training, they undergo repeated cycles of reincarnation. Confirming this fact is the very act of faith itself." According to this idea, faith is not something that began when humans started falling into hell. It is something more fundamental.

In fact, faith is the same as declaring who you are. How will you answer when someone asks you, "Who are you? Who is your family?" You will most certainly answer, "I'm a child of such-and-such family." Likewise, faith means to be able to answer, "I'm a child of God. God is my Parent. He is sometimes referred to as 'Buddha.'" So, knowing who you are is the beginning of faith.

Faith has existed even before hell was formed. Nevertheless, now that hell exists and an increasing number of people are falling there, it is all the more indispensable and necessary for people to have faith. In a nutshell, faith is like a lifeline. Humans are trying to return to their Parent—the Origin—by climbing up the rope of faith. So, ever since hell was created, it has become even more urgent and extremely important to spread faith.

Faith is a precondition for human existence

This may sound like a paradox, but the more comfortable this world becomes, the easier it becomes for people to lose faith. As civilization developed and life became convenient, like in the current age, this world has become a more comfortable place to live in. That is when people are likely to forget the blessings they received.

It is almost certain that Japanese people from thousands of years ago, such as during the Yayoi Period and the Jomon Period, believed in gods. However, a few thousand years later, in present-day Japan, people who are regarded as the most intellectual do not have faith, such as those who won the fierce competition to enter medical school and became professors of medicine after graduation. As a matter of fact, they think that humans are mere machines. They believe that the brain is the ruler of humans and that when it stops functioning is the end of one's life.

There are sometimes cases where a person gave birth to a child months after her brain had stopped functioning. Doctors claim that a dead person gave birth to a child, but if you think about it, is that really possible? Can a dead person really give birth to a child? Of course, not. Even so, doctors misunderstand these cases because they do not have a spiritual perspective. Since they believe that humans are the same as machines, they make claims like, "A machine is dead once its central processor breaks down. The same is true with humans. Once the brain stops working, they are dead. So, brain death means death." Even after they witnessed a person giving birth to a healthy baby several months after being brain dead, they still say that she is dead and do not see the truth.

There are people with similar views in other countries as well, such as in Europe and the United States. Most people believe in the existence of the soul, but even so, they consider a child born with anencephaly (a congenital defect where a baby is born without essential parts of the brain, like the cerebrum) as a nonhuman because it lacks a brain. Doctors often say, "It is not a human because it doesn't have a brain. It is not alive. It is dead. It is just a corpse," and easily put an end to a baby's life. This is truly horrific. People who do not know the truth can do something so terrifying like that.

This shows that people in the modern age have become "clever fools"—the more clever they get, the more foolish they actually become. They may have acquired a lot of knowledge, but they do not know the crucial truths. They do not know the most important and basic truths that appear on the first page of their "workbook of life."

Faith has existed from the very beginning; it is a precondition for human existence. Humans are allowed to live as humans on the condition that they have faith. Those who have lost sight of this premise have gone to hell, a place they did not need to go in the first place.

Save the living people first

At Happy Science, we are trying to save the souls who have fallen into hell by offering religious rituals such as memorial services for ancestors. But this is a way of playing catch-up, as we were too late in saving them before they passed. We must extend a helping hand while people are still alive.

If you have faith and live righteously in this world, you will not need to go to hell. So first, it is essential for those who are still alive to firmly hold onto their faith. All the major religions of the world provide teachings for the living. They do not provide teachings for the dead. So first, save the living people. Then, they will not face problems after they die. It is important to save the living first. That is the reason religions provide teachings.

In modern-day Japan, more than half the people are falling into hell after death. This is the current situation. So, we need to spread our teachings to the extent that everyone in Japan has read at least one of my books, heard at least one of my lectures, or attended at least one of our seminars at Happy Science. Then, the number of people who fall into hell will drop dramatically to 20 to 30 percent. Perhaps it may even drop down to 10 to 20 percent. What is more, if the world becomes filled with people who read and study many books of Truth, put those teachings into practice, and strive to make other people happy, most people will not have to go to hell.

This is not a goal too difficult to achieve. It is rather easy, to be honest. What we need to do is to change people's sense of values. People need religious faith. In other words, they need to be aware that God exists and that humans are God's children. Live in a way that God's children should live. Just by doing so, you will not have to suffer in hell. It is not difficult to put this into practice.

You just need a little more push. Teach people the Truth and encourage them to live by it. Then, they will not need to go to hell. Many souls are suffering in hell for hundreds of years, all because they do not know the Truth. It is so sad that I cannot bear to watch them. Even those who had a good social status in this world and lived a normal life have fallen into hell and are suffering because of their ignorance. However, people who can possibly end up in hell can be saved if you make efforts to teach them the Truth.

How can you take responsibility for all of humankind or for your entire race? It is by spreading the Truth, in other words, doing missionary work. You need to teach people the Truth while they are still alive. It is very difficult to save them after they die.

In conclusion, faith has existed from the very beginning of time. Faith means to confirm the fact. It also means that when someone asks you, "Who are you?" you can say, "I am a child of God." I hope to fill this world with people who can confidently say that.

7
The Relationship between Faith and Miracles

[Question]
Is there any place in Japan where miracles frequently occur based on faith, like the Lourdes Spring in France?

May Seminar held on May 3, 1990
at Takarazuka Grand Hotel in Hyogo, Japan.

The miracles of Lourdes have nothing to do with the location or the water

Lourdes is a place where the Virgin Mary had appeared, and as proof of this, healing miracles started to occur. In truth, however, the water of the Lourdes Spring has nothing to do with the miracles occurring there. The ingredients of the water have nothing to do with them, either.

A great number of people visit there, but the actual rate of illness being cured does not amount to even one percent. The number of cases is, in fact, extremely small. Among the many who visit Lourdes Spring, only a few experience miracles out of necessity. Miracles occur according to the will of the heavenly world. Not everyone will be cured.

What kinds of people experience miracles? The first are those who are meant to serve as living proof of God's existence. The second are those who are expected to accomplish great work following a miracle. Miracles occur to people who meet either of these conditions.

Alexis Carrel (1873-1944), a laureate of the Nobel Prize in Physiology or Medicine, wrote a book about the miracles of Lourdes. When he visited Lourdes Spring, he witnessed a severely ill person heal right in front of his eyes. Such a miracle happened because the heavenly world wanted him to write about it. He witnessed with his own eyes that a person with a terminal illness recovered completely, so he wrote about it, which then spread across the world. So what is truly happening at Lourdes is that high spirits who are linked with the spring are causing miraculous phenomena to promote missionary work. They make miracles happen for people whom they think are necessary, but not for others.

Your question is whether there is a place like that in Japan, and my answer is yes. In fact, miraculous phenomena often occur among local religions. There are local religions in villages, towns, or cities of rural areas, such as those that worship the gods of water. These religions often possess something that is considered holy, such as "healing water." Sometimes, illness can be cured by using such a thing, but this is not because the water itself possesses power. Among the guardian gods or guiding spirits of those religions, some are in charge of performing miracles; they are the ones who make decisions over whether to bring a miracle or not. So, in reality, factors like location, water, trees, and sand have nothing to do with miracles. Those things work as means to connect you to the spirits, so material things, themselves, are not directly associated with miracles.

Faith is the driving force behind miracles

The supporting or guiding spirit groups of a religion can perform miracles at any time and any place they want. But they are wise and do so after careful consideration.

At Happy Science, too, we get many reports of miraculous phenomena occurring in various places, but we do not necessarily highlight them. For example, some people were cured of their illnesses just by watching a video of my lecture. To be frank, a lot more miracles would certainly occur if we shifted the focus of our activities to performing miracles. Nonetheless, we do not take this approach. This is because if miracles occur frequently, the believers will stop studying the Truth. They will mostly be interested in miracles, become absorbed by them, and neglect studying as a result. That is why we refrain from making miracles happen too often.

If too many miracles occur, people in this world will become captivated by them and expect them to happen all the time. For this reason, the supporting spirits or guiding spirits control the number of miracles that occur. If the supporting or guiding spirit group is fully committed to performing miracles, anything is possible. But since the third-dimensional world is different from the Spirit World, miracles are only allowed for exceptional cases, and the way they happen is mostly up to the spirits' decisions. Of course, the spirits would want to bring miracles to those with faith. This is only natural. So, you can say that faith is the driving force behind miracles.

In reality, spirits in the other world do sometimes respond to the calls from people on earth. If, for example, after I return to the other world, I hear someone who strongly believes in me keep calling my name earnestly, I might well make an appearance in this world. I may appear, thinking, "I'm quite busy, but since they are calling for me so desperately, I'd better go see them." But if the person is calling me only half-heartedly, I probably will not come down. I might just think, "It seems like the issue will soon be solved, so I guess I don't need to bother going there." This is how things are. Faith is indeed the strong driving force to draw power from the other world.

CHAPTER FOUR

Love Blows Like the Wind

Recorded in Japanese on December 16, 2003
at Happy Science's General Headquarters in Tokyo, Japan.

1
The Truth About the Greek God Hermes

The true image of Hermes is only taught at Happy Science

The Happy Science movie *The Golden Laws* (Executive Producer Ryuho Okawa) was released in Japan in October 2003, and it was also shown in other countries. After watching the movie, overseas viewers commented that they wanted to know more about God Hermes, who appeared in it. So, I decided to talk about Hermes in this chapter. The movie also depicts Jesus Christ and Moses, but I think many people are already very familiar with them. On the other hand, they probably know Hermes only as one of the Twelve Olympians in Greek mythology. This cannot be helped because that is how he has been portrayed to this day.

Happy Science describes Hermes differently from how he is depicted in Greek mythology. Of course, no one else has explained Hermes in the way I do, so my description of him is completely original to Happy Science. Therefore, I certainly understand why people were surprised to see Hermes in the way he was depicted in our movie and said,

"I'm not familiar with that version of Hermes. That was new to me." It is only natural that people felt that way.

I once wrote a story about Hermes by recollecting my memories from my ancient past life.* It was made into a series of books with the same title as this chapter, *Love Blows Like the Wind* (a four-volume series published by IRH Press). Since they are not yet translated into other languages, many people overseas may not know about the story. But the story was made into a movie under the title *Hermes—Winds of Love*, and was released both in Japan and abroad in 1997. It is a new "Greek mythology"—a new legend of a hero that was revived in this modern age.

A leader who was active long before Zeus

So, how is Hermes portrayed at Happy Science? The story dates back 4,300 years. Unlike what is commonly told in Greek mythology, Hermes lived long before Zeus. I have said in my other books that Hermes was born and active about 4,300 years ago, which is several hundred years before Zeus was born.

---

* Refer to the section, "Who Is El Cantare" on p.172-173.

In the Greek mythology we know today, almost all the gods are described as children of Zeus. But that is simply impossible, and I am sure that people today would agree, too. In the myth, Zeus is portrayed as a figure with an extremely human-like side to him. In fact, when the Greeks compiled the myth, they made up a story of Zeus taking on many wives, who then bore many gods, one of whom was Hermes. But the truth is that there was a leader called Hermes who founded his religious group, and several hundred years later, Zeus appeared and established his own religious group. I believe the followers of Zeus rewrote Greek mythology, centering it around Zeus.

Notable features of Hermes

I would like to start by talking about what Hermes did. Hermes was born on the island of Crete in Greece, located in the Mediterranean Sea, and his birth town, now called Sitia, was in the eastern part of the island. He was a hero who aspired to unify Greece with a foothold in Crete.

Hermes had several distinctive features, one of which was that he strongly emphasized love in his teachings. This means that the teachings of love were already taught mainly in the Mediterranean region more than 2,000 years before

Jesus Christ was born. This fact in itself carries a significant meaning from a philosophical point of view.

The second feature I should mention is that he taught the philosophy of the Spirit World and explained the other world in great detail. In the Greek myths we know today, Hermes is described as a messenger between the Spirit World and this world. This is one of the traces of the fact that he spoke a great deal about the Spirit World when he was living in this world. As a matter of fact, Hermes was able to travel freely between this world and the other world. This phenomenon is often called an out-of-body experience—a person's soul temporarily leaves the physical body to experience the Real World and then returns. In the modern age, Emanuel Swedenborg (1688-1772) from Europe reported similar experiences. This is another feature of Hermes.

The third notable feature of Hermes is that he was the god of commerce, as has been handed down to this day. At a port in Amsterdam, in the Netherlands, there is a replica of an 18th-century cargo ship with a statue of Hermes standing on the stern. People have placed his statue there with the wish to make their business prosper. In Japan, too, schools that focus on teaching business often have statues of Hermes. In this way, Hermes is still known to this day as the god of economy and prosperity. This is because he was the one who came up with the idea of the Mediterranean trade and worked to develop it fully. The island of Crete is located approximately in the center of the Eastern Mediterranean Sea, which is south of mainland Greece and north of Egypt. Taking advantage of this location, Hermes conducted trade with inland Europe and North Africa, while basing himself in Crete. You can say that this prosperity in the Mediterranean region later led to the prosperity of Europe.

2

Hermes Was Also Revered as a God in Egypt

The only Greek god in Egyptian mythology

Perhaps many of you are still not fully convinced that Hermes was the central figure among the many Greek gods. However, there is proof that what I am saying is true. It is in the legends that are handed down in Egypt, a neighbor of Greece located across the Mediterranean Sea. It is said that the peak of Egyptian civilization was from approximately 2,000 years before the birth of Jesus Christ to the time of Cleopatra in the first century BC. This period mostly overlaps with the peak of Greek civilization. When you examine the Egyptian myths and legends of those times, you will find that only one Greek god makes an appearance, namely, Hermes. The Egyptians knew that Hermes was a Greek man. They were also aware that Hermes, who had left this world and had become a spiritual being, was guiding the Egyptian people from the Spirit World. They believed that Hermes of Greece was guiding them in the religious sense.

The peak of Egyptian civilization, which was between 2,000 BC and the first century BC, was a time when various pharaohs (kings) emerged. What is known as the "Age of the Pyramids" also belongs to this time. This period coincides with the period when the Greek gods were born and active on earth. These "gods" were, in fact, human beings living in the same time period as the great Egyptian pharaohs. This is why the Greek gods do not appear in Egyptian mythology, except for Hermes.

The time when Zeus and the Twelve Olympians were playing an important role in Greece overlaps with the time when Egypt was seeing much development and prosperity through the construction of pyramids. Because they all lived in the same period, the Egyptians did not acknowledge Zeus and others as gods. Hermes was the only god-like figure revered by the Egyptians.

Hermes and Thoth guided Egypt from the Spirit World

What is more, the Egyptians firmly believed that Hermes from Greece was none other than the ancient God Thoth, who was known as the god of wisdom in the early days of Egyptian civilization. God Thoth was a god worshiped during the early stage of Egyptian civilization. Paintings depicting Thoth can be found on the walls of the ancient Egyptian ruins.

According to the spiritual research of Happy Science, Thoth was a leader who was born on the continent of Atlantis, which has already disappeared from the face of the Earth. Those who had escaped from Atlantis and settled in Egypt worshiped God Thoth. The ancient Egyptians believed that Thoth, the god of wisdom who guided Egypt, was later reborn in Greece as Hermes. They also believed that Hermes and Thoth worked together as one in the Spirit World and guided Egypt, especially in the religious sense, to bring about more than 2,000 years of prosperity. This is not just a myth but a historical fact that is clearly recorded in the Corpus Hermeticum. (A collection of ancient Greek philosophical and religious texts, attributed to Hermes Trismegistus.)

The Egyptian people understood Thoth as a god who used a scale of spiritual values to weigh and record the good and bad in a person's soul in the Spirit World. They believed that God Thoth weighed and recorded the amount of good and evil people had done during their lives and decided their destination in the afterlife. For this reason, they feared God Thoth. The common feature of Thoth and Hermes was that they both had a strong will to guide this world from the Spirit World.

The concept of resurrection originated in Egypt

The philosophies of Thoth and Hermes have been handed down in Egyptian religion as the concept of resurrection, which is the idea that the dead will be reborn, in other words, come back to life. However, people misinterpreted this idea and believed that preserving a person's body as a mummy, instead of cremating it, would allow their soul to return to the body and come back to life. So, they believed that the soul of the pharaoh would one day return to his mummified body. This is how they interpreted the concept of resurrection.

This Egyptian idea led to the Christian idea of resurrection, namely, the resurrection of Jesus. In Christianity, people believe that Jesus was resurrected after being crucified. In the Bible, it is described as if Jesus was resurrected in the physical sense, but I believe it was rather a spiritual resurrection. This concept of resurrection did not originate in Christianity, but it actually began in Egypt.

The modern Swiss philosopher Carl Hilty (1833-1909) said that the concept of resurrection is the core idea of Christian teachings, and I think he is right on that score. If it were not for the idea of resurrection, Christianity would have been nothing but a story of Jesus being crucified and executed along with other criminals. Christianity, which has lasted for over 2,000 years, would not have been established if the story simply ended with Jesus being abandoned by his twelve disciples and dying on the cross, despite having done missionary work with them. The fundamental reason Christianity has spread throughout the world and has become a major religion lies in the idea of resurrection. Without it, Jesus would have simply been a man who died as a political and ideological criminal, and Christianity would not have been able to exert spiritual influence to a great extent.

It is said that many people witnessed the resurrection of Jesus. According to the Bible, more than 500 people witnessed it. So, quite a lot of people of his time must have seen him. The Bible describes that it was the resurrection of his physical body and that one of Jesus' disciples, Thomas, was even able to touch his wounds. Leaving aside the question of whether it was a physical resurrection, at the very least, it is true that Jesus appeared before his disciples as if he were still alive. His disciples must have seen him that way. This belief in the resurrection of Jesus Christ became the starting point of the salvation movement in Christianity.

Nonetheless, as I mentioned earlier, the idea of resurrection itself came from Egypt, and the Egyptian religious philosophy was created by two spiritual beings, Thoth and Hermes, who are actually one and the same. This is what lies at the root of the Christian idea of resurrection. Therefore, if you explore the roots of Christianity, you will see that Hermes' philosophy has flowed from Greece, Egypt, and then to Israel. This is my understanding of the idea of resurrection, which is part of mysticism.

3

A Being That Has Responsibility over Both This World and the Other World

The differences between Hermes and Jesus Christ

Jesus Christ taught love just as Hermes did, but in slightly different ways. When Jesus taught about love, he placed the greatest emphasis on love for God. He taught people to love God, whom we cannot see, and to love our neighbors as proof of our love for God. Jesus did not expect much from this world. The kingdom of God, or the kingdom of heaven, that he sought was not of this world; the true land of souls or utopia he sought existed in the world beyond this one.

In contrast, Hermes, who was active in Greece about 2,000 years before Jesus, taught love differently. The philosophy of love he taught encouraged people to practice love and realize utopia in this world as proof. Although Jesus had given up on building utopia in this world, Hermes aspired to build utopia in this world as well as in the other world. As mentioned earlier, Hermes was a spiritual person with extensive knowledge about the Spirit World, but he also thought incredibly rationally, which enabled him to succeed in this world. This is because he was born into a royal family and was raised to be a king. The same can be said of Gautama Siddhartha (Shakyamuni Buddha), who was a reincarnation of Hermes in later history. So, due to his upbringing, Hermes had the ability to achieve a great deal in this world.

Hermes was a man of love, but he also had the ability to lead an army. Moreover, he had the power to bring prosperity to the people and the wisdom to enrich their lives. In other words, he brought wealth into people's lives and spiritually enriched their minds while they lived in this world. Thus, it may be more accurate to say that Jesus was only able to deliver half of the teachings Hermes preached. This may have something to do with the way they lived in this world. Comparing their lives on earth, Hermes was a man of completion who ultimately accomplished his work in this world, whereas Jesus was a man of tragedy who left this world at the young age of 33.

Unique features of El Cantare

Whether or not a religious leader can complete his work in this world depends on how rational the person is. Most people who are religious and spiritual have a mystical, unworldly way of thinking and lack rational thinking. It is extremely difficult to balance both rational thinking and mystical thought, so most people lean toward one or the other. However, Hermes had both a mystical and a rational side to him. The same was true with Gautama Siddhartha, who was a reincarnation of Hermes. He, too, had both mystical thoughts and rational thinking of this earthly world. This is one of the features of the soul that was born as Hermes and Gautama Siddhartha. In other words, this particular soul has responsibility over both the other world and this world.

Simply teaching people about attaining happiness in the other world or the next life is already enough of a mission for a religion to fulfill. However, some religious leaders took things even further and dared to make efforts to change this earthly world into a happy, utopian world. There is no doubt that the souls of these great figures embody the Will of the Being who originally planned and created the system of reincarnation for humans. This means there exists a Spiritual Being who is trying to realize happiness that can be carried over from this world to the other world. At Happy Science, we call this Being *El Cantare*. El Cantare has responsibility over both this world and the other world.

4
Love Is like the Clear Wind

Balancing "spiritual thoughts" with "thoughts of prosperity"

Based on what I have discussed so far, you may now understand that our big goal is to balance and harmonize spiritual thoughts with thoughts of worldly progress and prosperity. It is true that people who are spiritual and who live for love tend to be naive and not very successful in this world. On the other hand, people who prosper economically and achieve worldly success often seem to forget about spiritual senses or love, and instead, live at the mercy of their selfish desires or desires for self-preservation. So it seems as though people with a stronger ego or stronger desire for self-expansion tend to succeed more easily in this world. Many people probably have this impression.

In other words, people who are more inclined to this world appear to achieve success easily in this world. It appears as though people who strongly seek to become rich, to be promoted, to attain a higher position, and to have power over others are more likely to get ahead in this world. On the contrary, religious people seem to be choosing to give up on worldly success and instead set their hopes on happiness in the afterlife. In this context, we could say that being spiritual includes the attitude of giving up on this world. However, Hermes dared to take on the difficult challenge of finding the balance between being spiritual and being successful in this world.

The "clear wind" means love

What made it possible for Hermes to find the balance between these two themes? The answer is the idea that lies at the core of Hermes' philosophy, also symbolized by the expression, "Love Blows Like the Wind"—the title of this chapter. Hermes taught:

Love is like the clear wind. It comes from nowhere, blows past us, and travels on. It is invisible, so we have no way of seeing it. Even so, the wind is what it is precisely because it blows. If it were to stop blowing, it would no longer be wind.

Hidden in this thought is an important key What does the expression the "clear wind" mean? The answer is "love."

In the United States and Europe today, people seem to think of love as something that must be expressed in a tangible way. They believe that their partner would not be satisfied unless they clearly express their love. They believe that love between a husband and wife must be expressed in a concrete form for it to be real. So they confirm their love for each other by giving gifts, eating dinner together, or constantly telling each other that they love them. They do not understand love unless it is expressed in words. If words are not enough, they express it through actions such as hugging and kissing. They do not understand or feel satisfied with their partner's love unless it is expressed in a tangible way. When they cannot confirm it, they say things like, "I can't believe that you really love me" to their partner. This is likely how most couples behave in the West.

However, this is a visible form of love. It is love that people can see "who loves whom" with their eyes, and love that can be confirmed by a third party. For example, a husband might give his wife a ring or necklace and take her out for an elegant dinner at a hotel to demonstrate his love. A father may play baseball with his son on the weekend, or always go to watch him play to show his love. In this way, people express their love through concrete action. They think that they cannot say they love someone unless they show affection. That is why there are married couples who easily get divorced when they find that their partner no longer shows affection like they used to. This is an unfortunate situation. I must say that these people have almost no spiritual intuition.

The work of angels is transparent love itself

Why did Hermes teach a clear, wind-like love? Please think about this. What is it that is clear or transparent? Expressed differently, it is the spirit body, the spirit, and the soul. I want you to think about these existences.

Most of you probably cannot see the spiritual beings of the other world. Perhaps, some of you have thought about your guardian spirit and the light of angels who are always trying to help you and guide you. You may have thought about them as "concepts" in your head. But here, take a moment and put yourself in the shoes of these spiritual beings. Although you cannot see them, they are trying to save you. They are trying to help you so that you can be happy. They are trying their best to encourage you and guide you from the other world so that you do not choose the path to unhappiness. They also fight for you when you do wrong and come under the control of evil spirits or satans. In reality, they are making every effort, day and night, to bring you happiness. Even so, you cannot see them. You cannot even tell whether they exist or not. That is why you do not even thank them.

When I teach you about love, I would like to mention the following. In this world, love, indeed, can only be expressed in a visible form. However, this will change when you eventually leave this world and return to the other world. If you manage to avoid falling into hell and instead successfully return to heaven as a light of angel or an angel-to-be, what do you think your work will be? It will be to become the transparent love itself.

Your presence will not be visible to the people in the earthly world. You will not be thanked or appreciated by them, either. They will not know about the work you are doing. Even so, you will continue to care for them, wish for their happiness, and pour your passion into helping them. This act is what we call "love that blows like the clear wind." You will eventually become this kind of existence. If you cannot recognize this love yourself, you will never be able to become an angel, as such work of love is exactly what the angels are doing.

Who in this world recognizes this work of angels? Who knows about it? No one does. No one knows that angels are guiding people in churches or comforting people in war-torn places. No one knows that angels are working hard to create world peace. They are engaged in many activities. Many angels are working hard. Even so, no one in this world can see what they are doing. They are transparent love itself.

Nevertheless, they do not stop working. Even if people in this world do not understand their work, do not acknowledge their existence, or even if people deny their existence and say, "Angels don't exist. The other world doesn't exist. Spirits don't exist," angels continue to help the people in this world. Just like the wind, they travel through the world selflessly. They will never be seen by others. Only the feeling that they passed by will remain in people's hearts. Their wish to make people happy manifests through the actions of the people in this world. This is the love of angels. So, the love that blows like the clear wind, which Hermes taught, was essentially the love of angels.

An unconditional love that seeks nothing in return

We talked about the love of angels. Then, what is human love? As I mentioned earlier, human love is a visible form of love. Of course, you may be putting in effort to love others, but are you sure you are not always seeking something in return? There must be a part of you that is always seeking something in return. A husband may love his wife, but he naturally expects her to love him back. The same goes for a wife who loves her husband; she naturally expects something in return. You may be giving love to your neighbors, but you are probably expecting them to return the favor. Is this not true?

A lot of people are involved in various volunteer work, but more often than not, a part of them seeks the recognition that comes with it. This means that what people recognize as actions of love in this world may not be considered real love from the perspective of the Spirit World. Of course, even though people may expect something in return, taking those actions is still better than doing nothing at all; it is important to be kind and helpful to others. However, if the acts of love contain selfish motives and self-preserving desires or are conducted out of the wish to benefit oneself, that love becomes like a wind that carries sand. It is just like a sandstorm; dust is mixed in the clear wind. This is the nature of your love when you act out of self-serving motives.

The love of angels is not that kind of love. Their love is a love of devotion, a love that gives, and an unconditional love. Their love is one-directional. They simply keep giving. They do not expect anything in return. Although a person can appear to be doing something good in this world, if he or she is expecting praise from others, asking for promotions, or expecting money in return, that is not the love of angels in the truest sense.

Creating utopia in this world as well

The love that Hermes taught was the love of angels. Based on this unconditional love, Hermes aspired to create utopia in this world as well. He aspired to build an ideal world and aimed to develop and bring prosperity to this world. Hermes did not give up on this world. He had a strong wish to create a harmonious world in this earthly world, too. These were Hermes' attitudes.

A world of happiness already exists in the afterlife, in the other world. The other world is divided into two major realms, heaven and hell. Heaven is a place where souls who are filled with light and happiness reside. People whose minds were filled with light and good thoughts when they were alive will return there. Then, what about hell? It is a place for people who lived only for themselves and their own selfish desires. They felt it was normal to benefit themselves at the cost of others and thought nothing of hurting others, killing others, or ruining others' lives. They only cared about their own well-being. These people fall into hell after death. So, there are two major realms in the other world.

The world of heaven is filled with happiness; it is a utopia. So, if returning there is the only goal of humans, things would be simple, indeed. However, the reason why hell exists lies in this earthly world. Hell is created by people's wrong ways of living and thinking in this world. So, unless we strive to make this world an ideal place, hell will never disappear. If we do not accomplish this in our current lifetime, we will simply be postponing it to our next lives.

Angels are carrying out their work of salvation in the other world as well. They go to the world of hell—or what Christians call purgatory—to save the souls suffering there. This is a very tough spiritual training for angels, but they are working very hard every day. I am determined to create many people who awaken to the Truth and strive to create utopia on earth. I am doing this because it can also lighten the burden on these angels.

5
Awaken to the Enlightenment of Earthlings

The teachings that encompass the philosophies of Hermes and Buddha

The teachings of Happy Science encompass the philosophy of Hermes in Greece and the philosophy of Buddha in India. These two are our core ideas.

Happy Science has built many *shoja* (temples) around Japan, starting with Sohonzan Shoshinkan (a head temple in Utsunomiya City, Tochigi Prefecture). When you look at these shoja, you can tell that many of them are built based on Greek architecture. It is said that the roots of a religion become obvious when the group constructs its own buildings. If you look at our buildings, you will clearly see that Happy Science has its origin in Greece. However, inside these Greek-style buildings, we are practicing Buddhist-style, or Indian-style, spiritual training. This is the true nature of Happy Science.

As you can see, Happy Science has Hermes-like aspects on the outside and Buddha-like philosophy on the inside. I hope you can understand that this is the current state of Happy Science.

Happy Science aims to become a global-scale religion that integrates the East and the West

Happy Science is aiming to accomplish something even Jesus Christ was not able to do, which is to integrate and harmonize two different concepts—love and progress—and to manifest them in this world. What is more, we strongly encourage people to seek enlightenment to refine their souls as humans, undergoing spiritual discipline in this world. This idea has a strong Buddhist touch, which I think is lacking in the West.

Hermes became the source of Western philosophy, and Shakyamuni Buddha is the core figure of Eastern philosophy. In fact, these core philosophies of the East and the West both originated from the same Spiritual Being called El Cantare. When humankind learns this Truth, they will have no choice but to awaken to the enlightenment of Earthlings. I want people to know that the West and the East share the same origin. I am now trying to unify and integrate the two philosophies that have developed separately, and create the next global-scale religion.

Currently (2005), Christianity and Islam are starting to conflict with each other. Buddhism no longer has enough power to save people, either. Religion is essentially what divided people into different races. Since religion divided them into races, religion must also work to unify these races.

I began the activities of Happy Science so that all human beings on Earth can live in a world of happiness as members of a utopian society. I sincerely hope that many people will support this idea and join this new movement of salvation.

Afterword

According to Greek mythology, God Hermes has the mission to relay messages from the Spirit World. As I reread this book, I feel that I, too, have the same significant duty to fulfill. I am well-versed in the state of affairs of the other world, or the Spirit World. I have spoken with many spirits and even traveled to the dimensions beyond this one numerous times to experience it for myself. And I have continuously been weaving the wisdom I gained from my abundant experiences in the Spirit World into the systematic teachings of Happy Science as a single piece of fabric or cloth—in other words, the Laws. This is a truly, truly wondrous work that carries an important mission from heaven.

As you read through this book, you will gradually see Buddha, Hermes, and El Cantare emerging as one figure. I have been trying to convey the existence of El Cantare, who had been unknown to many of you, repeatedly and in many different ways. El Cantare is the Being with the missions of Buddha and Hermes in other words, integrating the principles of the East and the West—who is trying to guide humanity as a whole.

The teachings of El Cantare are now being taught in this small island country, Japan, located in the Pacific Ocean, and they are now reaching all over the world. My teachings are being translated into many different languages, and each of my books has been read by people of various nationalities. Every day, this Truth is spreading. I am sure that these teachings will prevail all across the Earth within the next century. They shall continue to spread for 2,000 or 3,000 years to come and be appreciated for embodying the principles that can keep guiding many generations of humankind.

Yes, the Being, who had been guiding the numerous Light of Guiding Spirits and Light of Angels who were born in this world and preached many teachings and philosophies over several millennia of human history, has now appeared and is trying to reveal His Real Teachings. The Truth that you are now witnessing is infinitely deep and has existed from the infinite past and will continue to exist into the infinite future. I would like you to learn this Truth accurately and convey it now, so that the people in later generations can learn it, too.

I am the Love you believe. I am the Truth you believe. I am the Road you seek. I am the Hope you desire. Your Lord is the One and Only. Your Lord is El Cantare. Please walk forward tirelessly on this Road to El Cantare.

Ryuho Okawa
Master & CEO of Happy Science Group
Spring 2005

For a deeper understanding of
Invitation to Faith
see other books below by Ryuho Okawa:

The Mystical Laws [Tokyo: HS Press, 2015]
The Laws of the Sun [New York: IRH Press, 2018]
The Golden Laws [Tokyo: HS Press, 2015]

ABOUT THE AUTHOR

Founder and CEO of Happy Science Group.

Ryuho Okawa was born on July 7th, 1956, in Tokushima, Japan. After graduating from the University of Tokyo with a law degree, he joined a Tokyo-based trading company. While working at its New York headquarters, he studied international finance at the Graduate Center of the City University of New York. In 1981, he attained Great Enlightenment and became aware that he is El Cantare with a mission to bring salvation to all humankind.

In 1986, he established Happy Science. It now has members in 186 countries across the world, with more than 700 branches and temples, as well as 10,000 missionary houses around the world.

He has given over 3,500 lectures (of which more than 150 are in English) and published over 3,250 books (of which more than 600 are Spiritual Interview Series), and many are translated into 42 languages. Along with *The Laws of the Sun* and *The Laws of Hell*, many of the books have become best sellers or million sellers. To date, Happy Science has produced 28 movies under his supervision. He has given the original story and concept and is also the Executive Producer. He has also composed music and written lyrics for over 450 pieces.

Moreover, he is the Founder of Happy Science University and Happy Science Academy (Junior and Senior High School), Founder and President of the Happiness Realization Party, Founder and Honorary Headmaster of Happy Science Institute of Government and Management, Founder of IRH Press Co., Ltd., and the Chairperson of NEW STAR PRODUCTION Co., Ltd. and ARI Production Co., Ltd.

BOOKS BY RYUHO OKAWA

THE CHALLENGE TO ESTABLISHING THE IMPERISHABLE TRUTH

NOW IS THE AGE OF SPIRITUAL AWAKENING

ISBN: 978-1958655399 • $17.95

As an authority on spiritual matters and the afterlife, Ryuho Okawa invites readers to embrace a spiritual view of life by explaining how the roughly 30,000 days we spend on earth shapes our destiny after death. A life grounded in goodness and gratitude leads to tenfold happiness in the next world, while self-centered living draws the soul toward unhappiness.

Okawa further teaches that the true purpose of education is to seek the Truth and nurture the soul. Recognizing that all people are spiritually connected—like branches of a great tree of life—forms the foundation for giving love.

The Eternal Truth described in this book will become the foundation for a new value system in the coming age of spiritual awakening.

Recommended Titles

THE LAWS OF THE SUN

ONE SOURCE, ONE PLANET, ONE PEOPLE

ISBN: 978-1-942125-43-3 • $15.95

How was this world created, and why do humans live in this world? *The Laws of the Sun* answers life's questions humans have always had throughout history. In this book, Ryuho Okawa outlines the laws that govern the universe and provides a road map for living one's life with greater purpose and meaning. The Truth taught in this book will significantly transform your life and allow you to develop love and acceptance toward people of all races and religions.

THE LAWS OF ETERNITY

EL CANTARE UNVEILS THE STRUCTURE OF THE SPIRIT WORLD

ISBN: 978-1-958655-16-0 • $17.95

Where do we come from, and where do we go after death? *The Laws of Eternity* answers life's most important questions that we are all confronted with at some point or another. Author Ryuho Okawa takes us on a journey to the other world, a place where we came from before we were born and return to after death. Open its pages and discover the eternal mysteries and the ultimate secrets of Earth's spirit group that have been covered by the veil of legends and myths.

THE LAWS OF FAITH

ONE WORLD BEYOND DIFFERENCES

ISBN: 978-1-942125-34-1 • $15.95

In this book, Ryuho Okawa preaches the core teachings of the world religion and the faith in the God of Earth. By integrating logical and spiritual viewpoints, Okawa gives answers to modern-day problems that traditional religions cannot solve. Through this book, you will learn to go beyond different values, harmonize with each other and between nations, and create a world filled with peace and prosperity.

THE MYSTICAL LAWS

GOING BEYOND THE DIMENSIONAL BOUNDARIES

ISBN: 979-8-88737-038-5 • $14.95

"I believe that once you have finished reading this book, you will find it impossible to return to your old self, for you have now learned the secrets that run through this world and the other.

When you have learned of what has been hidden, will you feel guilt or will you find courage welling up from within?"

-From the Afterword

WHAT IS HAPPY SCIENCE?

BEST SELECTION OF RYUHO OKAWA'S EARLY LECTURES (VOLUME 1)

ISBN: 978-1-942125-99-0 • $17.95

The Best Selection series is a collection of Ryuho Okawa's passionate lectures from the ages of 32 to 33 that reveal the mission and goal of Happy Science. Volume 1 teaches the eternal Truth, including the meaning of life, the secret of the mind, the true meaning of love, the mystery of the universe, and how to end hatred and world conflicts.

THE WAY TO HUMAN PERFECTION

BEST SELECTION OF RYUHO OKAWA'S EARLY LECTURES (VOLUME 2)

ISBN: 978-1-958655-20-7 • $17.95

The path to enlightenment starts from understanding 'the eternal viewpoint of life.' By recognizing that we have eternal life, we can realize that caring and bringing joy to others are the keys to true happiness and success. By walking the path to higher enlightenment, we can cultivate our character and develop better relationship with others.

Be Infinitely Kind

For we are living in the Great River of Love

ISBN: 978-1-958655276 • $17.95

What is true love? What is the true definition of kindness? In this book, Ryuho Okawa invites readers to explore the deeper spiritual virtues of love and kindness—essential qualities for building strong, lasting relationships with those we hold dear. Truthfully, the more love we give, the wealthier our souls become.

The Origin of Love

On the Beauty of Compassion

ISBN: 978-1-941779-84-2 (ebook) • $14.95

Why do people love or hate each other? Ryuho Okawa answers this question by explaining the origin of love from the perspective of eternal life. When you truly understand love, you will awaken to the wonder of life and love for your neighbors.

The Laws of Happiness

Love, Wisdom, Self-Reflection and Progress

ISBN: 978-1-942125-70-9 • $16.95

Happiness is found within us, not outside. It is in how we think, view life, and work. This is an ultimate guide to becoming happy through the Fourfold Path of Love, Wisdom, Self-Reflection, and Progress—the universal law of happiness.

An Unshakable Mind

How to Overcome Life's Difficulties

ISBN: 978-1-942125-91-4 • $17.95

This book will guide you to build the genuine self-confidence necessary to shape a resilient character and withstand life's turbulence. Ryuho Okawa breaks down the causes of life's difficulties and provides solutions to overcome them from the spiritual viewpoint of life based on the laws of the mind.

THE TRUTH ABOUT EARTH, THE UNIVERSE, THE SPIRIT WORLD

LIFE'S Q&A WITH EL CANTARE

ISBN: 978-1-958655-26-9 • $17.95

A compilation of 28 Q&A sessions conducted by author Ryuho Okawa, where he answers numerous intricate questions varying from the theory of evolution to the creation of the multidimensional universe, all without a script.

KANJIZAI, BUDDHA'S OMNISCIENT POWER OF PERCEPTION

GOING BEYOND TIME, SPACE, AND THE GREAT UNIVERSE

ISBN: 978-1958655290 • $17.95

Kanjizai is a profound spiritual power that allows you to perceive all things. This book unveils what it means to possess real spiritual power—one that inspires humility, sincerity, and the pursuit of genuine enlightenment. *Kanjizai* is a guide to awakening your infinite potential as human being, unveiling the eternal truths of the universe and the Creator.

ONE MORE STEP FORWARD

THE INVINCIBLE THINKING TO GET YOU THROUGH TOUGH TIMES

ISBN: 978-1-958655-25-2 • $17.95

Success in life is determined not by our circumstances but by our mindset and how we think. In this book, author Ryuho Okawa reveals from his first-hand experience how the spirit of self-help can create new values. His drive to keep moving forward by taking steady steps has led to the publication of over 3,200 books in 37 years (at the time of its publication). Unlock the keys to lifelong growth and success.

TRUE BUSHIDO SPOKEN BY AME-NO-MIOYA-GAMI

THE JAPANESE FATHER GOD TEACHES HOW WE SHOULD LIVE AND DIE

ISBN: 978-4823304606 • $20.00

Nearly 30,000 years ago, Ame-no-Mioya-Gami (The Japanese Father God) descended on the foothills of Mt. Fuji in a fleet of spaceships. He taught the values of Justice, Prosperity, Order, and Harmony, which are the original Japanese spirit. In this book, Ame-no-Mioya-Gami speaks on the true meaning behind bushido and why people must regain the samurai spirit.

THE ESSENCE OF BUDDHA

THE PATH TO ENLIGHTENMENT

ISBN: 978-1-942125-06-8 • $14.95

The essence of Shakyamuni Buddha's original teachings of the mind are explained in simple words. Through this book, you will learn how to attain inner happiness, the wisdom to conquer ego, and to enter the path to enlightenment.

THE CHALLENGE OF THE MIND

AN ESSENTIAL GUIDE TO BUDDHA'S TEACHINGS: ZEN, KARMA AND ENLIGHTENMENT

ISBN: 978-1-942125-45-7 • $16.95

In this book, Ryuho Okawa explains essential Buddhist tenets and how to put them into practice. He offers a solid basis of reason and an intellectual understanding of Buddhist concepts.

THE LAWS OF GREAT ENLIGHTENMENT

ALWAYS WALK WITH BUDDHA

ISBN: 978-1-942125-62-4 • $17.95

Discover the power of forgiveness from Buddha's enlightenment and compassion, and the true relationship of work and enlightenment. In addition, the author reveals his own experience when he attained the Great Enlightenment.

THE ETERNAL BUDDHA

NOW, HERE, IS THE IMPERISHABLE LIGHT

ISBN: 978-1-958655-19-1 • $17.95

Embedded in this book is a message from Eternal Buddha, the parent of your soul. You will discover the true origin of your soul, why you have chosen to be born in this time, and why having faith is important.

THE TEN PRINCIPLES FROM EL CANTARE VOLUME I

RYUHO OKAWA'S FIRST LECTURES ON HIS BASIC TEACHINGS

ISBN: 978-1-942125-85-3 • $16.95

How did Happy Science begin? What are its teachings? What is its aim? This is a compilation of early lectures that built the foundation of Happy Science. The historic moments are captured in this book.

THE TEN PRINCIPLES FROM EL CANTARE VOLUME II

RYUHO OKAWA'S FIRST LECTURES ON HIS WISH TO SAVE THE WORLD

ISBN: 978-1-942125-86-0 • $16.95

Volume II contains passionate messages of Ryuho Okawa filled with the wish to save humankind and build utopia on earth. You can also learn about God's three major inventions, the mission of religion, and more.

WHO IS EL CANTARE?

El Cantare means "the Light of the Earth." He is the Supreme God of the Earth who has been guiding humankind since the beginning of Genesis, and He is the Creator of the universe. He is whom Jesus called Father and Muhammad called Allah, and He is *Ame-no-Mioya-Gami*, the Japanese Father God. He is also known as Vishnu in India and Tiandi in China. Different parts of El Cantare's core consciousness have descended to Earth in the past, once as Alpha and another as Elohim. His branch spirits, such as Shakyamuni Buddha and Hermes, have descended to Earth many times and helped to flourish many civilizations. To build a new civilization on Earth by uniting various religions and integrating various fields of study, a part of the core consciousness has now descended as Master Ryuho Okawa.

Alpha is a part of the core consciousness of El Cantare, who descended to Earth around 330 million years ago. Alpha preached Earth's Truth to harmonize and unify Earth-born humans and space people who came from other planets.

Elohim is a part of the core consciousness of El Cantare, who descended to Earth around 150 million years ago. He gave wisdom, mainly on the differences between light and darkness, good and evil.

Ame-no-Mioya-Gami (The Japanese Father God) is a Being who is close to the core consciousness of Lord El Cantare, and is the Creator God and the Father God who appears in ancient literature, *Hotsuma Tsutae*. It is believed that He descended on the foothills of Mt. Fuji about 30,000 years ago and built the Fuji dynasty, which is the root of the Japanese civilization. Ame-no-Mioya-Gami's Teachings spread to ancient civilizations of other countries in the world.

Shakyamuni Buddha was born in Nepal around 2,600 years ago as the prince of the Shakya clan. When he was 29 years old, he renounced the world and sought enlightenment. He later attained Great Enlightenment and spent most of his life in India teaching and practicing the Truth. He is the founder of Buddhism, which has spread extensively throughout Asia.

Hermes is one of the 12 Olympian gods in Greek mythology, but the spiritual Truth is that he taught the teachings of love and progress around 4,300 years ago, which became the origin of the current Western civilization. He is a hero who truly existed.

Ophealis was born in Greece around 6,500 years ago and was the leader who went on an expedition as far as Egypt. He is the God of miracles, prosperity, and arts, and is known as Osiris in Egyptian mythology.

Rient Arl Croud was born as a king of the ancient Incan Empire around 7,000 years ago and taught about the mysteries of the mind. In the heavenly world, he is responsible for the interactions that take place between Earth and various planets.

Thoth was an almighty leader who built the golden age of the Atlantic civilization around 12,000 years ago. In Egyptian mythology, he is known as God Thoth.

Ra Mu was a leader who built the golden age of the civilization of Mu around 17,000 years ago. As a religious leader and a politician, he ruled by uniting religion and politics.

ABOUT HAPPY SCIENCE

Happy Science is a religious group founded on the faith in El Cantare, who is the God of the Earth and the Creator of the universe. The true essence of human beings is an eternal soul created by God, and we go through the cycle of reincarnation to train and develop our souls. We have been carrying out various activities to spread this spiritual value and build a peaceful and prosperous world that God wishes. At Happy Science, we explore righteousness, in other words, God's Will. This is called the "Exploration of Right Mind." More specifically, it means to practice the Fourfold Path: Love, Wisdom, Self-Reflection, and Progress. This is the path that leads humans to attain happiness that carries over from this world to the next.

Love—practicing "love that gives"
To give love to others without expecting anything in return is the starting point of happiness. By practicing "love that gives," you will become closer to God.

Wisdom—studying spiritual truth
By studying the Truth, you will be able to distinguish good and evil, live righteously, and learn the heart of God. True wisdom leads people to true happiness.

Self-Reflection—correcting your mistakes
Self-reflection is the act of correcting wrongful thoughts and actions you have accumulated during the day and regaining the pure, true nature of the soul.

Progress—creating utopia on earth
True progress is about spreading happiness to others and improving society as you achieve your own success. This will create utopia on earth.

PLACES OF WORSHIP FOR HAPPY SCIENCE

Shoja

—A PLACE TO REFINE YOUR MIND, GAIN SPIRITUAL WISDOM, AND BE REBORN

Happy Science shoja (temple) is a sacred spiritual field where you can deepen your faith and heighten your enlightenment. Under the spiritual guidance of high spirits, shoja holds various seminars to improve individual character and practices ritual prayers to help believers solve their life problems and make progress. By participating in them, you can regain the peaceful and blissful mind that you may have lost in your everyday life.

29 SHOJAS IN JAPAN, 3 SHOJAS AND LA DOJO OVERSEAS

San Francisco

Local Branch

—A PLACE TO CHANGE YOUR DESTINY

Since 1986, Happy Science has been carrying out various activities to produce people who can truly say, "I am happy." At our local branches, many new believers are being born and are leading better lives through faith in Lord God El Cantare. All kinds of events take place here, such as lecture viewing, book seminars, prayers, and counseling sessions. Everyone is welcome!

HAPPY SCIENCE'S ENGLISH SUTRA

"The True Words Spoken By Buddha"

"The True Words Spoken By Buddha" is an English sutra given directly from the spirit of Shakyamuni Buddha, who is a part of Master Ryuho Okawa's subconscious. The words in this sutra are not of a mere human being but are the words of God or Buddha sent directly from the ninth dimension, which is the highest realm of the Earth's Spirit World.

"The True Words Spoken By Buddha" is an essential sutra for us to connect and live with God or Buddha's Will as our own.

MEMBERSHIPS

MEMBERSHIP

If you would like to know more about Happy Science, please consider becoming a member. Those who pledge to believe in Lord El Cantare and wish to learn more can join us.

When you become a member, you will receive the following sutras: "The True Words Spoken By Buddha," "Prayer to the Lord," and "Prayer to Guardian and Guiding Spirits."

DEVOTEE MEMBER

If you would like to learn the teachings of Happy Science and walk the path of faith, become a Devotee member who pledges devotion to the Three Treasures, which are Buddha, Dharma, and Sangha. Buddha refers to Lord El Cantare, Master Ryuho Okawa. Dharma refers to Master Ryuho Okawa's teachings. Sangha refers to Happy Science. Devoting to the Three Treasures will let your Buddha nature shine, and you will enter the path to attain true freedom of the mind.

Becoming a devotee means you become Buddha's disciple. You will discipline your mind and act to bring happiness to society.

EMAIL OR **PHONE CALL**

Please turn to the contact information page.

ONLINE member.happy-science.org/signup/

CONTACT INFORMATION

Happy Science is a worldwide organization with branches and temples around the globe. For full details, visit happy-science.org. The following are some of our main Happy Science locations:

UNITED STATES AND CANADA

New York
79 Franklin St., New York, NY 10013, USA
Phone: 1-212-343-7972
Fax: 1-212-343-7973
Email: ny@happy-science.org
Website: happyscience-usa.org

New Jersey
66 Hudson St., #2R, Hoboken, NJ 07030, USA
Phone: 1-201-313-0127
Email: nj@happy-science.org
Website: happyscience-usa.org

Chicago
33 West Higgins Rd. 4040,
South Barrington, IL 60010, USA
Phone: 1-630-937-3077
Email: chicago@happy-science.org
Website: happyscience-usa.org

Florida
5208 8th St., Zephyrhills, FL 33542, USA
Phone: 1-813-715-0000
Fax: 1-813-715-0010
Email: florida@happy-science.org
Website: happyscience-usa.org

Atlanta
1874 Piedmont Ave., NE Suite 360-C
Atlanta, GA 30324, USA
Phone: 1-404-892-7770
Email: atlanta@happy-science.org
Website: happyscience-usa.org

San Francisco
525 Clinton St.
Redwood City, CA 94062, USA
Phone & Fax: 1-650-363-2777
Email: sf@happy-science.org
Website: happyscience-usa.org

Los Angeles
1590 E. Del Mar Blvd., Pasadena,
CA 91106, USA
Phone: 1-626-395-7775
Fax: 1-626-395-7776
Email: la@happy-science.org
Website: happyscience-usa.org

Orange County
16541 Gothard St. Suite 104
Huntington Beach, CA 92647
Phone: 1-714-659-1501
Email: oc@happy-science.org
Website: happyscience-usa.org

San Diego
7841 Balboa Ave. Suite #202
San Diego, CA 92111, USA
Phone: 1-626-395-7775
Fax: 1-626-395-7776
E-mail: sandiego@happy-science.org
Website: happyscience-usa.org

Hawaii
Phone: 1-808-591-9772
Fax: 1-808-591-9776
Email: hi@happy-science.org
Website: happyscience-usa.org

Kauai
3343 Kanakolu Street, Suite 5
Lihue, HI 96766, USA
Phone: 1-808-822-7007
Fax: 1-808-822-6007
Email: kauai-hi@happy-science.org
Website: happyscience-usa.org

Toronto
845 The Queensway
Etobicoke, ON, M8Z 1N6, Canada
Phone: 1-416-901-3747
Email: toronto@happy-science.org
Website: happy-science.ca

Vancouver
#201-2607 East 49th Avenue,
Vancouver, BC, V5S 1J9, Canada
Phone: 1-604-437-7735
Fax: 1-604-437-7764
Email: vancouver@happy-science.org
Website: happy-science.ca

WORLDWIDE

Tokyo
1-6-7 Togoshi, Shinagawa,
Tokyo, 142-0041, Japan
Phone: 81-3-6384-5770
Fax: 81-3-6384-5776
Email: tokyo@happy-science.org
Website: happy-science.org

London
3 Margaret St.
London, W1W 8RE United Kingdom
Phone: 44-20-7323-9255
Fax: 44-20-7323-9344
Email: eu@happy-science.org
Website: www.happyscience-uk.org

Sydney
516 Pacific Highway, Lane Cove North,
2066 NSW, Australia
Phone: 61-2-9411-2877
Fax: 61-2-9411-2822
Email: sydney@happy-science.org

Sao Paulo
Rua. Domingos de Morais 1154,
Vila Mariana, Sao Paulo SP
CEP 04010-100, Brazil
Phone: 55-11-5088-3800
Email: sp@happy-science.org
Website: happyscience.com.br

Jundiai
Rua Congo, 447, Jd. Bonfiglioli
Jundiai-CEP, 13207-340, Brazil
Phone: 55-11-4587-5952
Email: jundiai@happy-science.org

Seoul
74, Sadang-ro 27-gil,
Dongjak-gu, Seoul, Korea
Phone: 82-2-3478-8777
Fax: 82-2-3478-9777
Email: korea@happy-science.org

Taipei
No. 89, Lane 155, Dunhua N. Road,
Songshan District, Taipei City 105, Taiwan
Phone: 886-2-2719-9377
Fax: 886-2-2719-5570
Email: taiwan@happy-science.org

Taichung
No. 146, Minzu Rd., Central Dist.,
Taichung City 400001, Taiwan
Phone: 886-4-22233777
Email: taichung@happy-science.org

Kuala Lumpur
No 22A, Block 2, Jalil Link Jalan Jalil Jaya
2, Bukit Jalil 57000,
Kuala Lumpur, Malaysia
Phone: 60-3-8998-7877
Fax: 60-3-8998-7977
Email: malaysia@happy-science.org
Website: happyscience.org.my

Kathmandu
Kathmandu Metropolitan City,
Ward No. 15, Ring Road, Kimdol,
Sitapaila Kathmandu, Nepal
Phone: 977-1-537-2931
Email: nepal@happy-science.org

Kampala
Plot 877 Rubaga Road, Kampala
P.O. Box 34130 Kampala, Uganda
Email: uganda@happy-science.org

ABOUT IRH PRESS USA INC.

Founded in 2013, New York-based IRH Press USA Inc. is the North American affiliate of IRH Press Co., Ltd., Japan. The Press exclusively publishes comprehensive titles on Spiritual Truth, religious enrichment, Buddhism, personal growth, and contemporary commentary by Ryuho Okawa, the author of more than 3,250 unique publications, with hundreds of millions of copies sold worldwide. For more information, visit Okawabooks.com.

Follow us on:

- Facebook: Okawa Books
- Instagram: OkawaBooks
- Youtube: Okawa Books
- Twitter: Okawa Books
- Pinterest: Okawa Books
- Goodreads: Ryuho Okawa

NEWSLETTER

To receive book-related news, promotions, and events, please subscribe to our newsletter below.

irhpress.com/pages/subscribe

AUDIO / VISUAL MEDIA

YOUTUBE

PODCAST

Visit the above to learn more about Ryuho Okawa's books. Topics range from self-help, current affairs, spirituality, religion, and the universe.